FOURTH EDITION

Instructor's Manual with Test Bank to Accompany

EXPERIMENTAL PSYCHOLOGY

UNDERSTANDING PSYCHOLOGICAL RESEARCH

BARRY H. KANTOWITZ
BATTELLE MEMORIAL INSTITUTE

HENRY L. ROEDIGER III
RICE UNIVERSITY

DAVID G. ELMES
WASHINGTON AND LEE UNIVERSITY

Prepared by

BRADFORD H. CHALLIS
UNIVERSITY OF TORONTO

WEST PUBLISHING COMPANY
ST. PAUL   NEW YORK   LOS ANGELES   SAN FRANCISCO

COPYRIGHT © 1991 by   WEST PUBLISHING CO.
50 W. Kellogg Boulevard
P.O. Box 64526
St. Paul, MN 55164-1003

98 97 96 95 94 93 92 91   8 7 6 5 4 3 2 1 0

ISBN 0–314–83819–8   ∞

Contents

Preface

Experimental Psychology: Understanding Psychological Research is a superior text designed for an introductory lecture or laboratory course in experimental psychology. The fundamental concepts of experimental psychology are introduced and elaborated upon in the context of discussions of current research topics. The authors use an integrative approach. The important experimental topics are generally treated in more than one chapter, providing the student an opportunity to gain a better understanding and appreciation of the many topics of experimental psychology. The format of this text allows the instructor maximum freedom in organizing his or her own course.

Two ancillary works - an instructor's manual and a study guide - have been written to accompany the text. The instructor's manual is designed to assist the instructor with lecture preparation and testing. A unit for each chapter and appendix is provided in the instructor's manual. Each unit begins with a chapter outline and a list of key terms taken from the text. These are followed by answers to the discussion questions appearing at the end of each text chapter. Following these answers, a lecture suggestion relevant to a topic covered in the text is provided; references are provided along with the lecture suggestion. Next, a suggested demonstration is outlined, illustrating a concept discussed in the chapter. The demonstrations are simple to complete and generally require a minimum of classroom time. The remaining part of the unit provides testing materials. First, there are two experimental dilemmas requiring critical thinking and the application of concepts covered in the chapter. The experimental dilemmas are hypothetical research scenarios which may or may not contain some flaw in design, procedure, or interpretation of results; solutions to the dilemmas are provided. Following the experimental dilemmas is a set of multiple choice test questions and a set of true-false questions based on the material in the text. Whereas some of the questions are constructed to test the basic concepts covered in a chapter, other questions test for more specific information related to an experimental topic. Answers to the multiple choice and true-false items are presented along with each question. At the back of the instructor's manual are the page numbers in the text that cover the material tested by a particular multiple choice or true-false question. A number of essay questions addressing general concepts are provided at the end of each unit.

As a complement to Experimental Psychology: Understanding Psychological Research, this instructor's manual should be very helpful to the instructor during the preparation of lectures and the construction of tests.

Explanation in Scientific Psychology

Key Terms

a priori method
applied research
basic research
correlation
curiosity
data
deduction
description
diffusion of responsibility
empirical
experimentation
explanation
falsifiability view
functional
induction

intervening variables
method of authority
method of tenacity
observation
parsimony
precision
prediction
quasi-experiment
scientific method
self-correcting
social loafing
strong inference
testability
theory

Answers to Discussion Questions

1.   a.   "Men are better drivers than women."
      Although a high percentage of people queried agree with this statement, all beliefs were based on personal observations and the fact that the statement sounds reasonable a priori. (It might be noted that no other reasons for believing this are possible since scientific observation has shown this statement to be false.)
      b.   "Children who have siblings are not as well adjusted as only children."
      Very few people believe this, but the few who do base their belief on results from scientific studies. Common folk wisdom generally leads to the rejection of this idea.
      c.   "People who learn to play a musical instrument do better in school than those who do not."
      About half of the persons queried believe this statement and belief is always based on the a priori feeling that the statement seems reasonable.
      d.   "War is good for the economy."
      Belief in this statement is fixed using a variety of methods. Some people use the method of authority in that they have always heard that it is true. Others use an a priori approach whereby the statement is deemed plausible since unemployment declines during periods of war, etc. Still others claim knowledge of systematic studies showing the statement to be true.
      e.   "Pets have positive effects on the health of their owners."
      Again, belief is fixed by all imaginable methods. Personal observation, authority, and scientific data are all invoked as evidence for the truth of this statement.

2.   *The inductive approach to science is a "bottom up" enterprise whereby general observations are made in the hopes that some order will emerge out of chaos. There are no guiding principles used to direct research and thus observations often become confused and disorganized. The deductive approach, on the other hand, is a "top-down" process in which theories are proposed and tested directly. There is no random manipulation of variables. Rather, only those experiments which test theoretical predictions are considered worthwhile. Despite their differences, both the inductive and deductive approaches have the same goal -- namely explanation. An example where both approaches have contributed to the success of a science may be taken from chemistry. The inductive approach was dominant during the early stages of the science when general observations were recorded. Later, theory came into play with the construction of the periodic table. Not only did the periodic table provide a way of organizing existing*

knowledge, but it correctly predicted the existence of undiscovered elements. Clearly the science of chemistry could never have been as successful as it has without the influence of both of these approaches.

3. *Following the initial research on social loafing, a number of different explanations or theories of social loafing were proposed. For example, one theory proposed an allocation-of-effort account whereas another theory suggested a diffusion-of-responsibility explanation. Using the procedure called strong inference, researchers attempted to eliminate alternative theories. They designed experiments such that the outcome would provide evidence in support of one theory and at the same time falsify a different theory.*

   This eliminative procedure called strong inference has been used in social loafing research. In several experiments, for example, the allocation-of-responsibility account was pitted against the diffusion-of-responsibility explanation. In the experiments, a person was tested either alone or in a group. Contrary to the allocation-of-effort account, the results indicated that social loafing occurred only when a person was in a group. Consequently, researchers rejected the allocation-of-effort account and concluded that the diffusion-of-responsibility explanation was superior.

4. *Although some experimental psychologists feel that the time has come to try and use their knowledge for society's benefit, most would agree that the science is still too young for this to be a useful enterprise. Most of experimental psychology is still in the basic research stage where observations are being gathered and theories are beginning to be constructed and tested. Although the ultimate goal is the application of general principles in the real world, that is far from being a major concern at present. Rather, an attitude of "knowledge for knowledge's sake" prevails.*

5. *Skinner's article (1956) reflect the strong views of an inductive scientist; he argues that the collection and interpretation of data is of primary importance in the scientists pursuit of understanding behavior. Skinner insists that science does not progress through carefully designed experiments motivated by theories; rather, he suggests that science is often a disorderly and accidental process, and that theories are generally worthless in suggesting experiments.*

   In contrast to the more orthodox view of science offered in the book chapter, Skinner (1956), in his article, espouses a more eclectic and opinionated view of science and its methods. He suggests, for example, a number of principles of scientific practice, including such advice as "when you run onto something interesting, drop everything and study it" and "some people are lucky". Although Skinner's views are in some ways different from those offered in the chapter, many similarities exist: Does not the principle mentioned above simply reflect the importance of curiosity in science?

   On occasion, Skinner does suggest that the deductive method of science has been of value, in that planned experiments from valid theorizing have lead to significant scientific results. The article covers the range of issues discussed in the chapter in a very interesting and readable fashion.

Reference

Skinner, B. F. (1956). A case history in scientific method. American Psychologist, 11, 221-223.

Lecture Suggestion

Even though scientists themselves are not too concerned with the philosophical analysis of their research methods, there exists an entire domain of study dedicated to the philosophy of science. One philosopher in particular, Thomas Kuhn, has attracted the attention of experimental psychologists in recent years. In 1970 Kuhn published a book entitled The Structure of Scientific Revolutions that has had an enormous impact on both the philosophical and scientific communities. According to Kuhn science does not build cumulatively but is fundamentally discontinuous and characterized by what he calls "revolutions".

The basic scenario goes as follows. During periods of normal (nonrevolutionary) science, research is conducted within a scientific community that has a common paradigm. That is, its members agree upon the types of questions that should be studied and upon the types of techniques that should be used to study them. Knowledge is accumulated throughout periods of normal science in a fairly orderly fashion and is interpreted in light of the accepted theoretical framework. Problems arise, however, when normal science stumbles upon anomalous findings which are uninterpretable within the paradigm. When enough of these anomalies are discovered and attempts to reconcile them with the theoretical view fail, the science undergoes a revolution. The scientific community is fractured as a result of the demise of the paradigm and each subgroup adheres to various revised versions of the old theoretical framework. When an acceptable alternative paradigm emerges, the revolution ends as members of the scientific community switch allegiance from the old to the new view.

Since the publication of his original (1970) book on scientific revolution, Kuhn has clarified and revised his views elsewhere (e.g., Suppe, 1977). One major objection to Kuhn's earlier work was that the notion of a "paradigm" was used too loosely to be meaningful. Kuhn used the term in several ways which were not all compatible with one another. The term "paradigm" has now been replaced with two distinct ideas; exemplars, or concrete problem solutions accepted by the scientific community; and disciplinary matrixes which are shared elements within the community such as symbolic generalizations or commitments to particular models. The scientist obtains his or her disciplinary matrix from the study of exemplars and they largely determine the matrix. The function of normal science is to further articulate and extend the matrix whereas a revolution is marked by the acceptance of a new matrix.

References

Kuhn, T. S. (1970). The Structure of Scientific Revolutions. Chicago: University of Chicago Press.
Suppe, F. (Ed.). (1977). The Structure of Scientific Theories. Chicago: University of Illinois Press.

Demonstration Suggestion

As was discussed in the text, the notion of testability is a very important one where theories are concerned. The only real way we have of evaluating a theory is to try and disprove it, and theories that are not testable can never be disproven. Thus, theories that are untestable are useless to scientists. As a classroom exercise, have students evaluate the following statements in terms of testability. In order that this demonstration is useful in illustrating the importance of formulating very precise hypotheses, have students revise statements into more testable forms.

1.　Beagles are smarter than poodles.
2.　The United States would never have become actively involved in World War II in the Japanese had not bombed Pearl Harbor.
3.　Soccer players are better athletes than football players.
4.　College students consume more beer per capita than any other age group.
5.　Our actions sometimes reflect conscious intentions, but are usually governed by subconscious urges.
6.　African voters grow better in filtered than in direct sunlight.
7.　Jackson Browne is a better musician than Rod Stewart.
8.　The design of the Honda Prelude is superior to that of the Toyota Corolla.
9.　Diamonds are a good investment.
10.　You learn more information when studying for an essay test than when studying for a multiple choice test.

Experimental Dilemmas

1. A scientist theorizes that people who have blue eyes are more intelligent than people with brown eyes. In order to test the theory the scientist obtains a variety of intelligence measures for 30 blue an 30 brown eyed subjects. These measures include grade point average, scores on the WAIS test, and SAT scores. A comparison of measures between groups shows that the blue eyed subjects score higher on all tests than the brown eyed subjects. The scientist states that "the data prove that people with blue eyes are more intelligent than those with brown eyes". Do you agree or disagree with this statement? Why?

ANSWER: *Disagree. The statement is too strong. This small sampling of data supports the notion that blue eyed people are more intelligent, but theories may never be "proven". They may only be disproven.*

2. A researcher seeking a grant from a federal funding agency proposes a series of experiments in which the effects of temperature stress on task performance will be studied. Specifically, the researcher plans to test subjects in an environmental chamber which will either be cold (52oF), normal (72oF), or hot (92oF). Subjects will monitor a TV screen filled with letters and will press a button whenever a particular predetermined target letter is displayed. Performance is expected to change depending upon the temperature of the chamber. A reviewer at the funding agency recommends that the grant be denied since the letter detection task bears no outright similarity to any task performed in a real job situation. Do you agree with the reviewer's judgment? If not, why?

ANSWER: *No. Even though people might never actually perform a letter detection task per se in the real world, the mental processes involved in letter detection are similar to those used in applied settings. For instance, the attentional demands of the letter detection task are similar to those involved in a job requiring an observer to monitor a panel for alarm signals.*

Questions

Multiple Choice

1. Social loafing refers to the observation that people
    a. become unsociable when tired.
    b. often work less when in a group.
    c. are apathetic when socializing in a group.
    d. lose interest in meeting people.

ANSWER: *B*

2. You believe that you may have trouble getting a phone call through to California following a report of an earthquake since it seems likely that some lines may have been damaged by the storm. Your belief is based on the
    a. scientific method.
    b. method of authority.
    c. a priori method.
    d. empirical method.

ANSWER: *B*

3.   A characteristic weakness with the a priori method of fixing beliefs is that
      a.   it incorporates no empirical basis for fixing belief.
      b.   it offers no way of declining the superiority of one belief over another.
      c.   it generates beliefs that do not seem intuitively plausible.
      d.   both a and b

ANSWER: *D*

4.   The scientific method
      a.   relies upon systematic observation.
      b.   has no mechanism for discarding outdated theories.
      c.   emphasizes the importance of theory over data.
      d.   none of the above

ANSWER: *A*

5.   The procedure that provides the strongest bases for making causal statements about the cause of a behavior is
      a.   quasi-experimental.
      b.   experimentation.
      c.   correlation.
      d.   observation.

ANSWER: *B*

6.   The inductive scientist
      a.   believes that patterns of explanation will become obvious once enough data are collected.
      b.   uses theory to guide research.
      c.   is concerned with testing between conflicting predictions made by different theories.
      d.   both a and c

ANSWER: *A*

7.   The deductive scientist
      a.   is most interested in gathering data on a phenomenon for which no theoretical explanation has been offered.
      b.   emphasizes the empirical rather than the theoretical approach.
      c.   gathers data only within a guiding theoretical framework.
      d.   would rather collect data than generate theories.

ANSWER: *C*

8.   In comparison to true experiments, quasi-experiments
      a.   provide more control.
      b.   provide a stronger bases for causal explanations.
      c.   use natural manipulations.
      d.   all of the above

ANSWER: *C*

9. The two major functions of a psychological theory are _____ and _____.
    a. organization; testability
    b. organization; prediction
    c. prediction; precision
    d. induction; organization

ANSWER: *B*

10. An approach to science whereby observations are gathered in the hopes of testing theoretical explanations is considered
    a. precise.
    b. inductive.
    c. deductive.
    d. data oriented.

ANSWER: *C*

11. In summarizing the effects of several variables, theories often use hypothetical constructs called
    a. independent variables.
    b. dependent variables.
    c. intervening variables.
    d. control variables.

ANSWER: *D*

12. When relating two independent variables with two dependent variables, an indirect method involving an intervening variable requires _____ arrows.
    a. one
    b. two
    c. three
    d. four

ANSWER: *D*

13. The advantages of the indirect method of explanation involving intervening variable is apparent when relating _____ independent variable(s) and _____ dependent variable(s).
    a. one; one
    b. two; two
    c. five; five
    d. none of the above

ANSWER: *C*

14. According to the falsifiability view,
    a. if a prediction is supported by data, the theory is true.
    b. theoretical predictions are always false.
    c. positive support for theories is more important than negative support.
    d. good theories must be fallible.

ANSWER: *D*

15.   Theories may be evaluated in terms of _____.
        a.   parsimony
        b.   testability
        c.   precision
        d.   all of the above

ANSWER: *D*

16.   A theory whose predictions are misinterpreted from one researcher to the next is said to
        a.   be testable.
        b.   be parsimonious.
        c.   lack precision.
        d.   be provable.

ANSWER: *C*

17.   A theory that explains a wide variety of occurrences with very few explanatory constructs is said to
        a.   be correct.
        b.   have high heuristic value.
        c.   be parsimonious.
        d.   be precise.

ANSWER: *C*

18.   The criterion that better theories contain fewer statements or assumptions is called
        a.   empirical
        b.   hypothetical constraint
        c.   precision
        d.   parsimony

ANSWER: *D*

19.   Experimental psychologists do basic research
        a.   in order to establish a reservoir of data from which to build theories.
        b.   because their only interest is in applied problems.
        c.   in laboratory settings having no elements in common with the real world.
        d.   both a and c

ANSWER: *A*

20.   Basic research
        a.   is entirely different from applied research.
        b.   is less important than applied research.
        c.   has no elements in common with the real world.
        d.   can lead to improvements outside the laboratory.

ANSWER: *D*

21.   When relating basic and applied research, the psychologist is more concerned that the _____ are the same and less concerned that the physical situation is the same.
   a.   experimenters
   b.   underlying processes
   c.   subjects
   d.   independent variables

ANSWER: *B*

22.   Psychological analysis of thought and behavior involves <u>description</u>, <u>prediction</u> and <u>explanation</u>. The corresponding research techniques are
   a.   data, results and statistics.
   b.   surveys, case studies and experiments.
   c.   observation, correlation and experimentation.
   d.   data, surveys and observation.

ANSWER: *C*

23.   The deductive scientist emphasizes _____ , whereas the inductive scientist emphasizes _____ .
   a.   data; observations
   b.   data; theory
   c.   theory; analyses
   d.   theory; data

ANSWER: *D*

24.   Which of the following is true concerning inductive and deductive scientists?
   a.   Inductive scientists provide basic data upon which to build theories.
   b.   Deductive scientists try to bring order out of the mass of data collected by empiricists.
   c.   Most psychologists take both an inductive and deductive approach.
   d.   all of the above

ANSWER: *D*

25.   The best theories
   a.   bear little relation to observed patterns of data.
   b.   have high explanatory power but very little predictive power.
   c.   usually need to be amended when new empirical observations are reported.
   d.   none of the above

ANSWER: *D*

<u>True-False</u>

26.   Subspecialities within psychology are distinguished by their emphasis on different research techniques.

ANSWER: *T*

27.   The simplest way of fixing belief is the method of authority.

ANSWER: *T*

28.   If the only scientific goal were to relate one independent variable and one dependent variable, the indirect method provides the simplest account.

ANSWER: *F*

29.   The a priori method of fixing belief involves systematic observation.

ANSWER: *F*

30.   In a true experiment, the researcher manipulates an intervening variable.

ANSWER: *F*

31.   The scientific method of inquiry allows one to decide the superiority of one belief over another.

ANSWER: *T*

32.   In comparison to true experiments, quasi-experiments use natural manipulations such as age.

ANSWER: *T*

33.   All science uses both data and theory.

ANSWER: *T*

34.   The word empirical is derived from a Greek word meaning self-correcting.

ANSWER: *F*

35.   The inductive scientist is primarily concerned with theory.

ANSWER: *F*

36.   Science tries to explain the world by relating independent and dependent variables by means of control variables.

ANSWER: *F*

37.   The inductive scientist hopes that explanatory principles will emerge once data have been collected.

ANSWER: *T*

38.   Rate of bar pressing, volume of water drunk and thirst are all examples of intervening variables.

ANSWER: *F*

39.   The deductive scientist emphasizes the importance of data collection.

ANSWER: *F*

40.   A theory can be very precise and not able to be tested.

ANSWER: *T*

41.   A theory may be defined as a set of related statements that explains a variety of occurrences.

ANSWER: *T*

42.   Theories must be immediately abandoned when discrepancies arise between their predictions and actual data.

ANSWER: *F*

43.   A correlation technique might be used for the purpose of prediction or selection.

ANSWER: *T*

44.   Theories may be proven if a large amount of supporting data is collected.

ANSWER: *F*

45.   Experiments performed in psychology laboratory settings have very little to tell us about behavior in the real world.

ANSWER: *F*

Essay

46.   What do the inductive and deductive approaches to science have in common?

47.   What is a theory? How are theories evaluated?

48.   Distinguish between basic research and applied research and discuss how they relate to each other.

49.   Explain what is meant by the following statement: Scientific psychology is characterized by an approach that is empirical and self-correcting.

50.   Psychological analysis of thought and behavior involves <u>description</u>, <u>prediction</u> and <u>explanation</u>. Discuss this statement with respect to the study of behavior called social loafing.

51.   Outline the strengths and weaknesses of the research procedures of observation, correlation, quasi-experimentation, and true experimentation.

** Text Page References for Test Questions can be found in Appendix C

Research Techniques: Observation and Correlation

Discussions Questions

Key Terms

anthropomorphize	ex post facto research
case study	naturalistic observation
cause	participant observation
confounding	Pearson r
correlation	reactivity
correlation coefficient	subject variables
cross-lagged-panel correlation procedure	survey research
delimiting observations	truncated range
deviant-case analysis	unobtrusive measures
ethogram	unobtrusive observations
ethology	variable

Answers to Discussion Questions

1. *Some behaviors that mothers might exhibit regarding the baby that are independent of the baby's immediate needs are talking, smiling, eating, sleeping, crying, doing laundry, reading, and cooking. Behaviors that an infant might engage in when left alone include cooing, smiling, babbling, crawling, crying, sleeping, playing, and teething. When the mother and child are together they might engage in feeding, holding, talking, playing, crawling, crying, sleeping, and smiling. It is reasonable to expect that some of these behaviors will be observed more often when the mother and child are apart that when they are together and vice-versa. Extensive observation and tabulation of these behaviors would provide some information as to their relative importance, but this information would only be correlational and therefore would provide no causal relationships. For instance, one might observe that babies cry less when their mothers are present, but we could not conclude that the mothers' absence causes crying or that her presence causes crying to cease without more controlled measures.*

2. a) *In general, the death rates appear higher for countries in which larger numbers of cigarettes are consumed, though this relationship is not perfect.*

    b) *This graph shows a general positive correlation between cigarette consumption and deaths per million.*

c)

$$r = \frac{(11)(1691400) - (6640)(2260)}{[(11)(5440400) - (6640)2] \quad [(11)(601800) - (2260)2]}$$

r = .737

3. *No. One can never infer causation from correlation even if the correlation is a perfect one. Any number of other variables might be invoked to explain this correlation. For instance it could be that living conditions in certain countries such as Great Britain were more stressful at the time these data were collected. This would have lead to higher death rates and also to higher cigarette consumption.*

4. *Some variables that might be highly correlated without being causally related might include:*
   a) *age and number of pairs of blue jeans owned*
   b) *yearly income and number of credit cards used*
   c) *number of heatstroke victims and ice cream cone consumption*
   d) *amount of beer consumed and rock-n-roll album sales*
   e) *gasoline consumption and number of little league baseball games in a given month*
   One might employ one of several statistical analyses to assess causal relationships between these factors, including the cross-lagged-panel correlation procedure.

Lecture Suggestion

There has been some controversy in recent years as to how our attitudes affect our behavior. Some have argued strongly that attitudes have very little effect on behavior, although our intuitions tell us otherwise. The basis of this argument is that some studies have found very low correlations between our attitudes and behaviors corresponding to those attitudes. Does this mean that advertisers are wasting their time in trying to change our attitudes about their products in hopes of increasing their sales? Not necessarily. Evidence reported more recently suggests that there is a positive correlation between our attitudes and behaviors, although it is often small. For instance, Freedman and Tyler (1975) found a positive correlation of .27 between tolerant attitudes toward pornography and behaviors such as reading pornographic material and attending pornographic movies. They also observed that people professing positive views toward alcohol tended to drink themselves (.62). In addition those people who felt that vitamin supplements were important were likely to take vitamins (.52). Other researchers have reported that attitudes will have stronger effects as they become more specifically related to behavior. Weigel, Vernon, and Tognacci (1974) measured attitudes toward the environment in general, pollution, conservation, and the Sierra Club. Attitudes toward the Sierra Club were strongly correlated with behaviors toward the club (.58) such as contributing money. However, less specific attitudes such as attitudes toward the environment were less strongly related to behaviors in the Sierra Club (.17). As the attitudes became less directly related to the behavior of supporting the Sierra Club it had less impact on behavior.

References

Freedman, J. L. & Tyler, T. (1982). The relationship between attitudes and behavior. In J. L. Freedman, Introductory Psychology. Reading, MA: Addison-Wesley.

Weigel, R. H., Vernon, D. T. A., & Tognacci, L. N. (1974). Specificity of the attitudes as a determinant of attitude-behavior congruence. Journal of Personality and Social Psychology, 30, 724-728.

Demonstration Suggestion

Have everyone in the class give an estimate of the distance in miles from their homes to the university campus. Then have them give an estimate of the number of times they visit their homes during the course of one school session (semester, quarter, etc.). Having gathered this information have each student work through the exercise of computing a Pearson Product Moment correlation coefficient for these data. Chances are that there will be a strong negative correlation between the two measures. That is, the further away a student lives, the less likely he or she is to make trips home during the school session. Discuss the outcome with the class. This particular example is interesting because students will likely wish to postulate a causal relationship between the two variables even though such a conclusion should not be drawn from correlational data.

Experimental Dilemmas

1. A social psychologist interested in the effects of unemployment on alcohol abuse conducted the following study. He mailed questionnaires to the homes of workers who had been laid off from a local automobile plant. The questionnaires were mailed at various time intervals and the workers were asked to anonymously fill them out and return them. The questionnaires contained items designed to provide information as to the amount of alcohol consumed daily before and after the layoffs occurred. Fifty percent of the subjects completed and returned all of the questionnaires sent out during the course of the experiment. For those individuals who returned the questionnaires, the researcher found a positive correlation between alcohol consumption and length of unemployment of .87. That is, more alcohol was consumed as the period of unemployment progressed. In his report the researcher stated that "the conditions of unemployment produce a tendency for people to increase their alcoholic intake." If you were the editor in charge of deciding whether his work would be accepted for publication, what would your judgment be?

ANSWER: *The work should not be accepted for several reasons. First, since the experimenter did not receive replies from all of the unemployed workers, caution should be exercised in interpreting the results. It could be (for whatever reason) that people who do not drink are less likely to cooperate in psychological research. Thus the sample of subjects might be biased to include more heavy drinkers initially. Secondly, the researcher's statement that unemployment produces an increase in alcohol abuse is completely unfounded. Causal inferences should never be drawn from correlational data since some other variable(s) could be mediating to produce the correlation. Third, the experimenter could have used more sophisticated experimental procedures such as testing people who had not been laid off from the plant and comparing those responses with those of the unemployed workers. Also the experimenter could wait until some of his subjects are rehired and then compare alcoholic intake before, during, and after unemployment for the same subjects. This type of information would provide more insight into the relationship between unemployment and alcohol abuse.*

2. An Australian ethologist has been studying the behavior of kangaroos for the past several months. She discovered a group of kangaroos living approximately 100 miles from her home and she moved out into the brush area in which they were living. Taking great care to always keep a distance of at least 1/2 mile between herself and the animals, the researcher observed the behavior of the kangaroos for 97 consecutive days. She tabulated the most frequently observed behaviors and constructed an ethogram from her findings. The behaviors exhibited most often by the kangaroos included eating, hopping, boxing, sleeping, and grooming. She noted different patterns of behavior among males and females and also between adults and young kangaroos. Is there anything wrong with this ethologist's attempts at naturalistic observation?

ANSWER: *No.*

Questions

Multiple Choice

1. Descriptive information gathered by case study and survey procedures are often combined as part of a(n) _____ approach.
    a. experimental
    b. quasi-experimental
    c. naturalistic
    d. correlational

ANSWER: *C*

2. Which of the following is true?
    a. Most of the scientific enterprise is concerned with the building of theories and very little attention is given to observation.
    b. Science is a cumulatively building enterprise.
    c. A discrepancy between the prediction made by a theory and an observation made by a researcher is unresolvable.
    d. none of the above

ANSWER: *B*

3. Descriptive observation
    a. is most useful during the early stages of scientific inquiry.
    b. relates observations to one another scientifically.
    c. provides for the control of extraneous variables.
    d. does not take place in natural settings.

ANSWER: *A*

4. Basic problems that threaten the validity of scientific observations include
    a. reactivity
    b. errors of observation
    c. delimiting the choice of behaviors to observe
    d. all of the above

ANSWER: *D*

5. The research techniques employed by scientists
    a. guard against errors of perception.
    b. help to ensure that observations accurately reflect the state of nature.
    c. can never lead to powerful inferences concerning the relationship between variables.
    d. both a and b

ANSWER: *D*

6.   In naturalistic observation, the observer's presence may make the measures
        a.   comparative.
        b.   reactive.
        c.   correlational.
        d.   subjective.

ANSWER: *B*

7.   Correlation coefficients
        a.   vary from 0 to 1.0.
        b.   vary from -1.0 to 0.
        c.   vary from -1.0 to 1.0.
        d.   vary from -10.0 to 10.0.

ANSWER: *C*

8.   Deviant-case analysis attempts to minimize
        a.   errors of observation
        b.   the difficulties of making inferences
        c.   reactivity
        d.   statistical bias

ANSWER: *B*

9.   Which of the following is an example of a negative correlation?
        a.   Body weight increases as children get older.
        b.   The rate of heart attacks is directly proportional to yearly income.
        c.   Shoe size increases as height increases.
        d.   The likelihood of owning a baseball card collection decreases with age.

ANSWER: *D*

10.

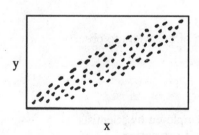

Which of the following correlation coefficients most likely corresponds to the pattern of data presented in this graph?
        a.   1.0
        b.   -.75
        c.   .70
        d.   .10

ANSWER: *C*

11. _____ occurs when two or more factors are varied simultaneously and leads to interpretational problems.
    a. Confounding
    b. Correlation
    c. Confliction
    d. Truncation

ANSWER: *A*

12. Eysenck and Evans (1981) argued that the correlation between lung cancer and smoking is produced by
    a. personality differences in humans.
    b. inordinately large doses of drugs given to laboratory animals.
    c. the mediation of a third variable.
    d. both a and c

ANSWER: *D*

13. In making scientific observations, "complete or pure objectivity" is only possible with
    a. the naturalistic approach
    b. experimentation
    c. deviant-case analysis
    d. none of the above

ANSWER: *D*

14. Low correlations
    a. imply a lack of causation between two variables.
    b. are found only with Pearson coefficients.
    c. may be produced by the truncated range of one of the variables.
    d. are seldom observed in psychological research.

ANSWER: *C*

15. The correlation coefficient does not measure
    a. the relationship between two variables.
    b. the direction of the relationship between two variables.
    c. the effect of one variable on another.
    d. the variation of one variable with another.

ANSWER: *C*

16. An experimenter computing the correlation between age and memory span would
    a. be able to show that old age produces a decrease in memory span.
    b. be able to determine that a third variable was involved.
    c. make an error because age and memory span are measured on different scales.
    d. none of the above

ANSWER: *D*

17.   Assessing the relation between two variables in correlational studies is usually made ex post facto, or
        a.   a priori
        b.   before the data are collected
        c.   after the data are collected
        d.   independently of data collection

ANSWER: *B*

18.   Before calculating a Pearson correlation coefficient it is advisable to plot the data because
        a.   one must be sure that the underlying relationship between the two variables is linear.
        b.   the diagram is more informative than the correlation coefficient.
        c.   one must make sure that the data are from a truncated range.
        d.   all of the above

ANSWER: *A*

19.   Scientists prefer to use _____ when determining the relationship among variables.
        a.   naturalistic observation
        b.   experiments
        c.   quasi-experiments
        d.   correlation

ANSWER: *B*

20.   The correlation coefficient that corresponds to a perfect correlation is
        a.   + 1.00
        b.   0
        c.   - 1.00
        d.   both a and c

ANSWER: *D*

21.   Using a cross-lagged-panel correlation procedure, Eron, Huesmann, Letkowitz, and Walder (1972) found evidence which suggests that
        a.   watching violent TV programs may produce later aggression.
        b.   aggressive people tend to watch violent TV programs.
        c.   people who watch violent TV programs when they are young continue to do so all their lives.
        d.   aggressive third graders watch violent TV programs when they grow up.

ANSWER: *A*

22.   In naturalistic observations, one can guard against reactivity by
        a.   making unobtrusive observations.
        b.   giving unobtrusive instructions.
        c.   taking unobtrusive measures.
        d.   both a and c

ANSWER: *A*

23. _____ is inherent in correlational research, and leads to interpretational difficulties with such research.
    a. Participant observation
    b. Reactivity
    c. Delimiting observation
    d. Confounding

ANSWER: *D*

24. A potential problem threatening the validity of naturalistic observations is that
    a. the observations are never reliable.
    b. the observer is unable to predict the participant's reaction.
    c. the participant may react to being observed.
    d. the observer can not statistically analyze the findings.

ANSWER: *C*

25. It is sometimes argued that experiments are merely controlled correlations because
    a. each manipulated variable is composed of more than one component.
    b. any one set of a variables components may cause an effect and we have no way of isolating all components.
    c. a certain amount of confounding is inherent in any experimental design.
    d. all of the above

ANSWER: *D*

26. Naturalistic observation is a valuable procedure in that
    a. it allows for extensive experimental control.
    b. it is easily replicated.
    c. it is primarily descriptive.
    d. it can define a problem area and raise further questions.

ANSWER: *D*

27. The correlational approach
    a. never involves ex post facto assessments.
    b. examines the degree of relationship between two variables.
    c. allows for causal inference.
    d. all of the above

ANSWER: *B*

28. Which of the following is true?
    a. We can rule out the possible effects of mediating variables in correlational research.
    b. As a correlation coefficient increases we can be more sure that a causal relationship exists between the two variables.
    c. It is not possible to correlate two variables that have different scales of measurement.
    d. none of the above

ANSWER: *D*

True-False

29.   Descriptive observation involves the recording of facts about natural phenomena.

ANSWER: *T*

30.   The correlational method provides for better understanding of events than any other scientific method.

ANSWER: *F*

31.   Naturalistic observation occurs mostly in laboratory settings.

ANSWER: *F*

32.   With recent advances in research techniques and equipment scientists can eliminate the possibility of errors of observation.

ANSWER: *F*

33.   Although firm inferences cannot be drawn from case studies, this problem is avoided with deviant case analyses.

ANSWER: *F*

34.   When the facts differ consistently and dramatically from the predictions, it is necessary to modify or abandon our theoretical conceptions.

ANSWER: *T*

35.   One advantage of naturalistic observations is that the researchers tend to anthropomorphize animal behaviors.

ANSWER: *F*

36.   We should view observation as secondary to experimentation because it lacks control.

ANSWER: *F*

37.   The ideal of objective observation in science may only be approximated.

ANSWER: *T*

38.   Case studies are representative of the overall population.

ANSWER: *F*

39.   Correlation coefficients vary between 0 and 1.0.

ANSWER: *F*

40.   Many naturalistic methods do not allow reproducibility.

ANSWER: *T*

41.   A positive correlation is observed if one variable increases as the other decreases.

ANSWER: *F*

42.   Only those variables with the same measurement scales may be correlated.

ANSWER: *F*

43.   Pearson's product-moment correlation coefficient and Pearson r are equivalent terms.

ANSWER: *T*

44.   If two variables are correlated one may predict the level of one variable given the value of the other variable.

ANSWER: *T*

45.   Possible mediation effects prevent the inference of causation from correlation.

ANSWER: *T*

46.   Confounding is a greater problem in experimental than in correlational research.

ANSWER: *F*

47.   An assumption underlying the Pearson r is that the relationship between two variables be linear.

ANSWER: *T*

48.   Correlation allows for more control of extraneous factors than does the experimental method.

ANSWER: *F*

49.   Inferring causation from correlation is more justified if a cross-lagged correlational procedure is used.

ANSWER: *T*

50.   Confounding is avoidable in correlational research.

ANSWER: *F*

<u>Essay</u>

51.   Why is correlation generally preferred to naturalistic observation? Give an example where naturalistic observation might be the preferable form of investigation.

52.   Describe how a scientist could investigate the claim that higher speed limits lead to more car accidents. Consider three different research techniques. Which one would you favour? Why?

53.   Discuss some of the problems inherent in interpreting correlation coefficients that are either very high or very low.

54.   Describe three basic problems that threaten the validity or soundness of scientific observations.

55.   Describe three different research techniques and outline the advantages and disadvantages of each of them.

** Text Page References for Test Questions can be found in Appendix C

Research Techniques: Experiments

Key Terms

Discussion Questions

Key Terms

abscissa	independent variable
baseline	interaction
between-subjects design	level
ceiling effect	matching
control conditions	mixed designs
control group	null results
control variable	quasi-experiments
counterbalancing	ordinate
critical experiment	randomization
data	random sampling
demand characteristics	regression artifact
dependent variable	regression to the mean
descriptive statistics	sampling
experiment	synergism
experimenter effects	what-if experiment
floor effect	within-subjects design
Hawthorne effect	

Answers to Discussion Questions

1. *One design for this problem would be to have half of the plumbers perform professors' work and half of the professors perform plumbers' work. Those plumbers and professors who are not performing the work of the other profession will either observe or offer advice to their "stand-ins." That is, the professor who is not doing plumbers' work will either observe the plumber trying to do the professors work, or will offer advice regarding the work. Similarly for the plumbers - they will either observe the professors trying to repair leaks or they will offer advice on how to do the work. The dependent variable might be based on some previously established number of tasks completed during a week, or on the number of assigned tasks for a specific week. Thus the professor might have 6 lectures, 3 committee meeting and 1 test to grade, while the plumber fixes 7 leaky sinks, installs 3 new faucets, etc. The dependent variable will be what percentage of these tasks are completed by the end of the week.*

    The independent variables are the type of work (plumbing vs. teaching) and activity of the observer (offers advice vs. observes quietly). Possible control variables might be age of subjects, sex of subjects, type of classes, type of plumbing tasks, etc. (Note that there are a myraid of possible control variables.)

    Results might show that the plumbers are able to complete (in one way or another) 80% of the tasks, and that advice vs. quiet observation had no effect. The professors might perform 50% of the tasks, and advice might greatly affect the percentage of tasks employed.

    Regarding design problems, this example illustrates design problems for virtually every aspect of an experiment, such as selection of dependent, independent and control variables, selection and assignment of subjects, etc. It also illustrates quite clearly that there are some problems that are extremely difficult to try and convert into an experiment.

2. *Situation A: If the principles of instrumental conditioning are used to increase the rate of responding with a dog over 7 years old, then no increase in rate of responding will be observed.*

   If a dog above the age of 9 years is deprived of food for 24 hours and then reinforcements are given following some behavior, then no improvements in that behavior will be observed.

   Situation B: If I increase my consumption of food purchased from fast food restaurants, then my GPA will decrease from the present level. If I purchase my breakfast, lunch and dinner from vending machines for one whole semester, then my GPA will be lower that semester than in previous semesters.

   Situation C: This cannot be translated into a testable hypothesis, since the "independent variable" of saved pennies is also the "dependent variable" of earned pennies. Students might, however, try to devise hypotheses such as "If a person saves more of their money, then they will have worked to earn more money." In this situation, one may consider the statement as a definition, and hence not testable. It is almost analogous to "A drop in temperature makes the air cooler."

   Situation D: If student study only the night before tests, then they will obtain higher test scores than if they study on several nights prior to the exam.

   Students who study only the night before the examination will always score on the average, higher than students who use any other study method.

3. *In a fictitious memory experiment, the two independent variables are the type of words used in the study list, (high-imagery words vs. low-imagery words) and the type of study instructions given to subjects (rote rehearsal versus instructions to form images of the words' referents.*

4. *An hypothesis is a particular prediction derived from a problem. The originator of an hypothesis derives the prediction from the problem, and hence is likely to believe the hypothesis itself. Since others have most likely not derived that hypothesis (or else there might already be one or more tests of the hypothesis), they are less likely to believe the hypothesis. The reason why an experimenter may not "believe" an experiment is because the experimenter, more than anyone else, is aware of all of the decisions that had to be made in order to conduct the experiment. Since there is no such thing as a perfect experiment, the person who makes the (sometimes arbitrary) decisions necessary to transform the hypothesis into an experiment is most likely to be cautious of the experiment.*
   (Note that the students may want to reconsider this statement after they have read Chapter Five, How to Read and Write Research Reports.)

5. *You might want to equate people on certain variables such as age, race, socio-economic status, level of education, and IQ. If this drastically reduces the size of the subject pool you could match experimental and control subjects of some of these variables in order to get a larger number of observations.*

Lecture Suggestion

The chapter points out that a better way to replicate an experiment than to repeat the same experiment is to extend the previous procedure by adding something new while retaining something old. By extending the original procedure part of the replication is a literal repetition, but the changed part of the experiment adds to scientific knowledge.

An example of how replication with extension can add to scientific knowledge is presented in the chapter. The example is drawn from the area of attention, and involves research using a dichotic listening task. In this task subjects are presented with separate words to each ear simultaneously. In one dichotic listening task, the split-span task, the subject is presented with a few items (e.g., words or numbers) to each ear, and is then asked to recall all of the items presented to both ears. Subjects may be asked to recall all of the items from either ear one at a time (i.e., recall all of the items presented to the right ear first then recall all of the items presented to the left ear), or pair-by-pair (i.e., recall the first item presented to the left ear, then the first item presented to the right ear, then the next item presented to the left ear, etc.). Early research showed that with slow item presentation rates (about one pair per second) the two recall methods (ear-by-ear and pair-by-pair) produced about the same recall performance levels.

When this early research was replicated, but now the items being presented at either a fast (two pairs per second) or a slow (one pair per second) rate, the data obtained with the slow presentation rate replicated the findings of the early research. However, the data from the fast presentation condition showed that recall by the ear-by-ear method was more efficient than was recall by the pair-by-pair method. These data were very important in formulating early models of attention (Broadbent, 1958).

Another dichotic listening task that provided data used in formulating the early models of attention was the shadowing task. In this task the subject is again presented with two messages, one to each ear. The subjects' task is to listen to one of the messages and repeat the words in the message as he hears them (i.e., shadow the message). The subject is to ignore the other message. When subjects are later asked what they remember from the unattended message, the usual finding is that they remember very little. Moray (1959), for example, showed that when a word was repeated as many as 35 times in the unattended message, the subjects did not remember these words.

Based on findings such as these Broadbent proposed his classic filter model of attention. One key aspect to this model is that it postulates that selective attention serves as a filter that only lets certain types of information be processed, and all unattended information is lost or forgotten. Thus in Moray's experiment, the attended message was processed so that the subject could shadow it, and the unattended message was lost from the information processing system.

A subsequent study that extended the usual shadowing experiment demonstrates how by extending procedures when we replicate experiments we can add to our scientific knowledge. Two Oxford University undergraduates, Gray and Wedderburn (1960), modified the split-span procedure and divided the two messages of different semantic categories between the two ears. For example, the message "Dear, six, Jane" was presented to one ear and "four, Aunt, one" was presented to the other ear. According to filter theory, when subjects are shadowing one message they should not be affected by the message in the unattended ear. However, Gray and Wedderburn's subjects often "switched" from ear to ear, and instead of shadowing "Dear, six, Jane" they shadowed "Dear Aunt Jane". This result showed that the semantic content of the unattended message was in fact analyzed (or else how could the subject have noted the word Aunt?), and was not lost, as predicted by filter theory.

References

Broadbent, D. E. (1958). Perception and communication. London: Pergamon.
Gray, J. & Wedderburn, A. (1960). Grouping strategies with simultaneous stimuli. Quarterly Journal of Experimental Psychology, 12, 180-184.
Moray, N. (1959). Attention in dichotic listening: Affective cues and the influence of instructions. Quarterly Journal of Experimental Psychology, 11, 56-60.

Demonstration Suggestion

In order to demonstrate some of the decisions that are involved in designing an experiment to solve some problem a useful demonstration is to design an experiment with the students' participation. Virtually any problem that can be translated into a testable hypothesis is appropriate for such a demonstration. The problem presented below is offered as a suggestion.

Stating the Problem:

Many words differ in the extent to which they refer to abstract concepts that cannot be directly experienced (e.g., democracy, innocence) as opposed to concrete objects, persons, things, and so (e.g., desk, apple) that can be felt, heard, smelled, or tasted. The general question being asked is whether or not the concreteness or abstractness of a word has any effect upon how easy it is to remember the word.

Translating the Problem into a Testable Hypothesis:
Are concrete words any easier or harder to remember than abstract words?

General Experimental Approach:
Present concrete and abstract words to subjects and see which type of words are easier to remember.

Independent Variables:
(a) Concrete versus Abstract words: How do we define concrete and abstract? How do we select words that are concrete words or abstract words? We can use published word norms (e.g., Paivio, Yuille, & Madigan, 1968, Toglia & Battig, 1978) to define concrete versus abstract words.
(b) There are a number of other ways in which words differ besides concrete versus abstract (e.g., word length, word frequency, pleasantness, etc.). Should we include one or more of these as an independent variable? What advantages or disadvantages are there to including one of these other variables as an independent variable?

Dependent Variables:
(a) free recall test?
(b) old/new recognition test?
(c) N-alternative forced choice recognition test?

Control Variables:
(a) word frequency
(b) word length
(c) list length (how many words are presented to the subjects?)
(d) presentation rate (at what rate are the words presented to the subjects?
Note that list length and presentation rate have a large effect upon how many words the subjects will be able to remember. You want to avoid making the task too easy (ceiling effects) or too difficult (floor effects) since this might obscure any effects of concrete versus abstract that might otherwise be obtained. Also, how might the type of dependent variable influence the selection of list length and/or presentation rate?

Experimental Design:
(a) within-subjects?
(b) between-subjects?
(c) mixed (if using more than one independent or dependent variable)?

Results:
It has been experimentally demonstrated that concrete words are easier to remember (when memory is tested by either free recall or recognition tests) than are abstract words (Paivio & Csapo, 1969).

References

Paivio, A. & Csapo, K. (1969). Concrete-image and verbal memory codes. Journal of Experimental Psychology, 80, 279-285.

Paivio, A., Yuille, J. C., & Madigan, S. (1969). Concreteness, imagery, and meaningfulness values for 925 nouns. Journal of Experimental Psychology Monograph, 76 (1, Pt. 2).

Toglia, M. P. & Battig, W. F. (1978). Handbook of semantic word norms. Hillsdale, NJ: Lawrence Erlbaum Associates.

Experimental Dilemmas

1. A researcher is interested in studying the effect of environmental stress on the performance of various mental tasks. The environmental stressor is the temperature level in the experimental chamber. The researcher selects three different temperatures (40∘F, 70∘F, and 95∘F) for the levels of stress to be included in the experiment. Since this is an experiment involving some risk to the subjects the researcher employs male undergraduates to serve as subjects. The mental task selected for the first experiment is a choice reaction time task in which one of four stimulus lights comes on and the subject is to respond by pressing one of four buttons as quickly as possible.

    The researcher thinks that stressful environments will make subjects respond faster. The researcher does not have a lot of money in his grant, so he decides to test each subject in each condition during the 90 minute testing session. Each subject is first tested in the 70∘ condition, then the 90∘ condition, and finally in the 40∘ condition. Each subject is given 30 trials in each condition.

    The results showed that the subjects mean reaction times for the three conditions were as follows:

Temperature	Mean Reaction Time
40∘F	430 msec
70∘F	525 msec
90∘F	487 msec

    Statistical analysis of the mean reaction times revealed that each of the three conditions was reliably different from the other two conditions. The researcher concluded that thermal stress improves reaction time. Do you agree with this conclusion? If not, why?

    ANSWER: *This conclusion should not be accepted for at least two reasons. First, the researcher only employed male subjects, and thus the results may not generalize to female subjects. Secondly, since the design used in the experiment was a within-subjects design, there may have been carryover effects. This seems especially likely in this case because the reaction times for the first, second, and third session were 525, 487, and 430 msec, respectively. Hence the improvement in reaction time could have been due to general practice effects and not to the effects of the thermal stress. Finally, it should be pointed out that in this experiment carryover effects besides simple practice effects might be a problem. For instance, after being tested in a 90∘F testing condition the subject might be perspiring, and this could easily affect how "stressful" the next testing condition (40∘) might be to the subjects.*

2. A counselling psychologist was interested in testing his hypothesis that physical exercise helps to alleviate depression. The psychologist was currently treating 39 people who were suffering from chronic depression. Thirty-six of these people said that they would be willing to participate in an experiment if the experiment might help them and might also provide information that would help the psychologist to learn more about how to help depressed people.

    The psychologist administered a standard paper and pencil test to measure how depressed his subjects were before treatment. The psychologist used these scores to match 12 groups of three people who scored about the same on the depression test. These three people were then randomly assigned to treatment conditions.

    People in condition I were asked to engage in some sort of outdoors exercise three times a week, people in condition II exercised five times a week, and people in condition III were not asked to exercise but they were asked to spend some time outdoors at least three times a week.

    At the end of the six week experiment the subjects took another paper and pencil depression test. The results showed that all subjects were now rated as less depressed then they were at the beginning of the experiment. However, the subjects in conditions I and II had improved more than the subjects in condition III. Subjects in conditions I and II had improved the same amount over the six week period.

The psychologist concluded that exercise provides help above and beyond that provided by simply spending time outdoors. He also concluded that three days of exercise a week was enough to benefit the depressed person. Do you agree with these conclusions? If not, why?

ANSWER: *Agree*

Questions

Multiple Choice

1.   In order to have an experiment, there must be at least _____ dependent variable(s), and at least _____ independent variable(s) with at least _____ level(s).
     a.   one; one; one
     b.   one; one; two
     c.   one; two; one
     d.   two; one; one

ANSWER: *B*

2.   Mixed design experiments manipulate independent variables
     a.   within-subjects.
     b.   between-subjects.
     c.   in a counterbalanced fashion.
     d.   both a and b

ANSWER: *D*

3.   In an experiment the _____ variable is a manipulation of the environment controlled by the experimenter.
     a.   control
     b.   experimental
     c.   dependent
     d.   independent

ANSWER: *D*

4.   One reason that a valid experiment may produce null results is
     a.   the levels of the independent variable are too similar to each other.
     b.   the dependent variable is subject to a floor effect.
     c.   extraneous variables are not held constant.
     d.   all of the above

ANSWER: *D*

5.   Failure of an independent variable to produce changes in a dependent variable is called a
        a.   statistical error.
        b.   failure to replicate.
        c.   null result.
        d.   confounding.

ANSWER: *C*

6.   In an experiment, the variable that the experimenter expects to change as a result of some
        experimental manipulation is termed the
        a.   dependent variable.
        b.   independent variable.
        c.   control variable.
        d.   experimental variable.

ANSWER: *A*

7.   A dependent variable is unreliable if it
        a.   does not yield the same score as it did previously when all conditions are the same.
        b.   is unaffected by the independent variable.
        c.   yields different scores for different subjects.
        d.   all of the above

ANSWER: *A*

8.   Floor and ceiling effects prevent
        a.   the influence of an independent variable from being accurately reflected in a dependent
              variable.
        b.   the influence of a dependent variable from being accurately reflected in an independent
              variable.
        c.   firm conclusions from being drawn concerning the effects of the independent variable.
        d.   both a and c

ANSWER: *D*

9.   The generality of an experiment is expanded by having more than one
        a.   intervening variable.
        b.   independent variable.
        c.   dependent variable.
        d.   both b and c

ANSWER: *D*

10.   Reasons for doing experiments with more than one independent variable include
        a.   demonstrating the generality of the effects of one independent variable.
        b.   they are more efficient than doing separate experiments with one independent variable each.
        c.   demonstrating interactions between the independent variables.
        d.   all of the above

ANSWER: *D*

11. That each person in an experiment has an equal chance to be assigned to any particular group is called
    a. counterbalancing.
    b. between-subjects design.
    c. randomization.
    d. matching.

ANSWER: *C*

12. An interaction can only be obtained when an experiment has
    a. more than one level of the dependent variable.
    b. more than one level of the independent variable.
    c. more than one dependent variable.
    d. more than one independent variable.

ANSWER: *D*

13. As the number of treatments increases, the number of orders for counterbalancing
    a. remains the same.
    b. increases.
    c. decreases.
    d. either a or b

ANSWER: *B*

14. A major disadvantage of between-subjects designs is that
    a. the effect of one treatment may alter the effectiveness of later treatments.
    b. subject differences may obscure treatment effects.
    c. one must use fewer independent variables.
    d. one can use only one dependent variable.

ANSWER: *B*

15. Some scientists are critical of "what-if" experiments because of the
    a. correlational approach.
    b. inefficiency.
    c. deductive approach.
    d. dependence on theory.

ANSWER: *B*

16. One reason for preferring randomization to matching for establishing group equivalence is that
    a. we do not know all the relevant variables to match.
    b. randomization involves more confounding.
    c. counterbalancing does not require randomization.
    d. randomization guarantees group equivalence.

ANSWER: *A*

17.   In within-subjects designs, counterbalancing is used to
        a.   enable the experimenter to evaluate possible treatment order effects.
        b.   assign subjects to treatment groups.
        c.   eliminate the effects of treatment order.
        d.   all of the above

ANSWER: *A*

18.   A mixed design is one in which
        a.   there is one independent and one dependent variable.
        b.   at least one independent variable is tested within- subjects and the other independent
             variable(s) is(are) tested between-subjects.
        c.   one independent variable is manipulated and the other independent variable(s) is(are)
             controlled.
        d.   each subject receives a mixture of treatment conditions.

ANSWER: *B*

19.   A control group or a control condition is included in an experiment to
        a.   evaluate experimenter effects and demand effects.
        b.   provide a baseline against which the variable of interest can be compared.
        c.   prevent ceiling or floor effects.
        d.   increase the generalizability of the results.

ANSWER: *B*

20.   Consider the following In an experiment designed to investigate the effects of alcohol on appetite:
        if drinks X and Y contain 0.5 and 1.0 ounces of vodka in orange juice, respectively, and drink Z
        contains only orange juice, then the control group in the experiment should receive
        a.   drink X.
        b.   drink Y.
        c.   drink Z.
        d.   nothing to drink.

ANSWER: *C*

21.   The Hawthorne effect is an example of
        a.   experimenter effects.
        b.   demand characteristics.
        c.   experimenter bias.
        d.   placebo effects.

ANSWER: *B*

22.   So-called critical experiments
       a.   test two theories that make different predictions.
       b.   test on theory that makes two different predictions.
       c.   involve an inductive approach.
       d.   involve a number of independent and dependent variables.

ANSWER: *A*

23.   Which of the following is true?
       a.   The dependent variable is observed.
       b.   The independent variable is constant.
       c.   The control variable is observed.
       d.   The independent variable is observed.

ANSWER: *A*

24.   Regression to the mean implies that if extreme scores are taken for some individuals and then the
       observations are repeated, the second scores obtained for these same individuals will be
       a.   closer to the mean of the first scores of the entire group
       b.   more extreme that the first scores of the selected individuals
       c.   less extreme than the first scores of the selected individuals
       d.   both a and c

ANSWER: *A*

25.   Which of the following is not a subject variable?
       a.   colour of hair
       b.   response time
       c.   sex
       d.   age

ANSWER: *B*

26.   Matching
       a.   is necessary for statistical reasons.
       b.   reduces the possibility of regression artifacts.
       c.   reduces the possibility of confounding of subject variables.
       d.   all of the above

ANSWER: *C*

27.   A control variable is
       a.   under the control of the subject.
       b.   a potential independent variable that is held constant.
       c.   varied in a controlled fashion by the experimenter.
       d.   a dependent variable that is held constant.

ANSWER: *B*

28.   An interaction occurs when the effects produced by
       a.   a dependent variable are not the same at each level of the independent variable.
       b.   one independent variable are not the same at each level of a second independent variable
       c.   one level of an independent variable are not the same at other levels of that independent
             variable
       d.   an independent variable are not the same at each level of the dependent variable

ANSWER: *B*

29.   The experimental problem of demand characteristics occurs when
       a.   subjects misinterpret the experimenter's instructions
       b.   the expectations of the experimenter influence the interpretation of the experimental results
       c.   the subjects' behavior is influenced by being in the experiment
       d.   there are treatment carryover effects

ANSWER: *C*

True-False

30.   In an experiment, the independent variable is a manipulation of the environment controlled by the
       experimenter.

ANSWER: *T*

31.   The following result is an example of an interaction: With normally active children, the stimulating
       effect of amphetamines increases as the dosage increases, but with hyperactive children the greater
       the dose of amphetamines, the calmer the children.

ANSWER: *T*

32.   In order to have an experiment it is necessary to have at least two levels of the dependent variable.

ANSWER: *F*

33.   The "control" in control variable refers to the fact that the variable is subject to controlled
       manipulation in the experiment.

ANSWER: *F*

34.   An experiment may produce null results because the experiment did not adequately control
       extraneous variation.

ANSWER: *T*

35.   Experiments are designed to permit statements about causation, such as independent variable A
       causes dependent variable B to change.

ANSWER: *T*

36.   One criterion for a good dependent variable is variability in repeated measures.

ANSWER: *F*

37.   Null results may occur because the experimenter did not produce a strong manipulation of the independent variable.

ANSWER: *T*

38.   Ceiling and floor effects are caused by using too extreme levels of an independent variable in an experiment.

ANSWER: *F*

39.   In order to obtain equivalent groups in between-subjects designs, you can use each subject as his or her own control.

ANSWER: *F*

40.   A control variable is a potential dependent variable that is held constant during the experiment.

ANSWER: *F*

41.   When the effects produced by one independent variable are not the same at each level of a second independent variable, we have an interaction.

ANSWER: *T*

42.   In between-subjects designs, you can attempt to match subjects on variables that are relevant.

ANSWER: *T*

43.   Results shown to be valid across several independent variables or several dependent variables are more valuable than data that has yet to be generalized.

ANSWER: *T*

44.   If an experimenter suspects that the effects of one treatment may linger on to alter a later treatment, then that experimenter should use a within-subjects design.

ANSWER: *F*

45.   An experiment does not need a dependent variable.

ANSWER: *F*

46.   The experiment by Brickner, Harkins and Ostrom manipulated the level of personal involvement and the level of personal identifiability.

ANSWER: *T*

47.   With a within-subjects design, counterbalancing techniques are used to eliminate the effects of treatment orders.

ANSWER: *F*

48.   In a quasi-experiment, subjects can be randomly assigned to all experimental conditions.

ANSWER: *F*

49.   When data are represented in figures, the dependent variable is represented on the ordinate and the independent variable is represented on the abscissa.

ANSWER: *T*

50.   Subjects in a quasi-experiment can be administered the same dependent measure.

ANSWER: *T*

Essay

51.   Design an experiment that examines the following claim: Pictures are remembered better than words and items studied once are better remembered than items studied twice. Outline the independent, dependent and control variables, and the experimental design.

52.   What are the advantages of using more than one independent variable? More than one dependent variable?

53.   Outline reasons for and against a quasi-experimental approach.

54.   Discuss the advantages and disadvantages of between-subjects and within-subjects experimental designs.

55.   Describe the advantages of experimentation over the other research techniques. What are the potential problems with experimentation? How are these problems avoided?

_____

** Text Page References for Test Questions can be found in Appendix C

Ethics in Psychological Research

Key Terms

aftercare   freedom to withdraw
confidentiality   informed consent
debriefing   protection from harm
deception   removing harmful consequences
ethical principles of the APA   speciesism

Answers to Discussion Questions

1. *The Casebook on Ethical Issues published by the APA makes for interesting reading, for it covers a variety of ethical complaints heard by the Ethics Committee. The cases deal with a range of issues concerning psychological research with animals and humans. As expected with such issues, arguments for and against the Ethics Committee's decision can be formulated. Although the specific ethical principles involved in each case differ somewhat, certain fundamental principles are common to many cases of a similar nature. For example, the types of ethical issues in socially sensitive research include some of the following: (1) privacy, (2) confidentiality (refers to data and not people, as with privacy), (3) deception, (4) informed consent, (5) justice and equitable treatment, (6) "ownership" of data, (7) soundness and validity of methodology, and (8) value or risk/benefit ratio of the research.*

2. *The listed articles describe ethical issues associated with different types of psychological research, covering such topics as AIDS, psychotherapy, socially-sensitive, and animal research. Several relevant articles are contained in the same issue of American Psychologist (1988; January issue), a journal which should be available in the University's library. Two specific issues covered in the articles include AIDS research and the study of race and gender variables. With AIDS research, confidentiality is a primary concern whereas with race and gender research, the risk/benefit issue is very important. On the other hand, certain general ethical principles (e.g. respect for the participants) apply in both areas of research.*

Lecture Suggestion/Demonstration

As with other scientific endeavours, psychological research can lead to ethical dilemmas. The text provides a number of examples, including the ethical dilemma that arose in the depression and memory experiment. Given the contentious nature of some psychological research, the issue of ethics in physical research lends itself to an open discussion or debate format. In this regard the instructor should consider consulting the book, Taking Sides: Clashing Views on Controversial Psychological Issues, by Rubenstein and Slife (1986). Many of the topics covered in the book are of an ethical nature, and the text provides opposing views. For example, one issue is whether deception in research can be justified? Stanley Milgram argues for the assertion and T. Murray argues against. The text also provides advice on implementing a debate format in the classroom. One approach is as follows:

The instructor or class select an ethical issue or a particular experiment with obvious ethical concerns (See the experimental dilemma for an example). The students are separated into two groups with one group defending the research and the other group arguing against the research on ethical grounds.

Reference

Rubinstein, J. & Slife, B.D. (1986). Taking Sides: Clashing Views on Controversial Psychological Issues. Guilford, CT: Dushkin.

Experimental Dilemma

1. A research is interested in the kinds of self-attributions people make about their own behavior and how
    those attributions govern behavior. The research proposed the following experiment. College students
    will be brought into a small seminar room for testing. The experimenter will tell them that they will
    receive several intelligence tests, and the better they do the greater the amount of credit they will
    receive for participation. Although the questions on the test will be extremely difficult, half the subjects
    will be told not to worry about the difficulty because the questions were devised for potential members
    of Mensa (an elite group of high IQ people). The other half of the students will be told that the test
    is a new version of a test to be used for admission to college. When students fail on most of the
    questions, the research will assess how the subjects' attribute their failure. A second aspect of the
    proposed study will be to videotape the subjects surreptitiously as they are completing the test.
    Subjects will be aware that the scoring manual for the test is in a book case in the testing room, and
    the experimenter wants to see how many students in each group cheats. Suppose you are on a
    committee that reviews the ethicality of research proposals. What would you say about the ethical
    aspects of this research?

    ANSWER: *The students should address the issues of deception and informed consent. Many aspects of
    the procedure involve deception, and the research has not made any provision for withdrawal,
    protection, or debriefing. Having a video tape of a student cheating, means that some provision
    for confidentiality must be undertaken.*

Questions

Multiple Choice

1.   One important principle advocated by the American Psychological Association is the right of
        informed consent, which states that the experimenter has a clear obligation to
        a.   obtain approval from a committee that judges the ethics of the proposed research before
                performing an experiment involving human subjects.
        b.   balance the potential worth of the research against the potential harm to the subjects prior to
                doing the experiment.
        c.   explain to the subjects all salient features of the research before the experiment is done so the
                subjects have the opportunity to decline to participate.
        d.   inform the subjects of the results of the research prior to publication of a journal article.

ANSWER: *C*

2.   Experiments involving deception
        a.   should never be done on ethical grounds.
        b.   should be carefully considered, since aftercare of the subject would be impossible to obtain.
        c.   obligates the researcher to explain the true nature of the experiment after the subject has been
                tested.
        d.   should only be conducted with infrahuman subjects.

ANSWER: *C*

3.   The view that animal life is somehow different from human life is called
        a.   racism.
        b.   speciesism.
        c.   stupidity.
        d.   bigotry.

ANSWER: *B*

4.   A research using animal subjects has an obligation to
        a.   use only innocuous independent variables.
        b.   engage in speciesism.
        c.   avoid the use of deception.
        d.   use human treatment.

ANSWER: *A*

5.   An important ethical obligation of a researcher using a drug as an independent variable is
        a.   to use only legal substances.
        b.   to use several different types of drugs.
        c.   to discourage students from doing drug research.
        d.   to guarantee adequate aftercare.

ANSWER: *D*

6.   Psychologists are primarily concerned with the ethics of research involving
        a.   paid subjects.
        b.   volunteer subjects.
        c.   animals.
        d.   all of the above

ANSWER: *D*

7.   During the initial stages of planning a future study, the _____ has the responsibility to make a careful evaluation of its ethical acceptability.
        a.   investigator
        b.   participant
        c.   research institution peer committee
        d.   granting agency

ANSWER: *A*

8.   Of primary ethical concern to the investigator is
        a.   the cost of the research.
        b.   the level of risk to the subject.
        c.   the value of the research to humanity.
        d.   all of the above

ANSWER: *B*

9.   The _____ always retains foremost responsibility to make a careful evaluation of the ethical acceptability of a study.
a.   granting agency
b.   university administration
c.   investigator
d.   scientific journal

ANSWER: *C*

10.   In a high-risk study, it is sufficient for the investigator to provide
a.   a simple debriefing.
b.   subjects with an appropriate phone number in case of problems.
c.   a guarantee of confidentiality.
d.   none of the above

ANSWER: *D*

11.   An ethical psychologist
a.   mistreats animal subjects.
b.   submits animal subjects to undue harm.
c.   ensures that all individuals using animals under their supervision have been instructed in the care of animals.
d.   none of the above

ANSWER: *C*

12.   The Ethics Committee of the APA educates _____ about ethical issues related to psychological research.
a.   psychologists
b.   the public
c.   students
d.   all of the above

ANSWER: *D*

13.   Except in _____ research, the investigator establishes a clear and fair agreement with research participants prior to their participation.
a.   no-risk
b.   minimal-risk
c.   high-risk
d.   both a and b

ANSWER: *D*

14.   The investigator is responsible for the ethical treatment of research participants by
        a.   collaborators.
        b.   students.
        c.   employees.
        d.   all of the above

ANSWER: *D*

15.   Information obtained about a research participant during the course of a study
        a.   is not confidential.
        b.   is always confidential.
        c.   is confidential unless otherwise agreed upon in advance.
        d.   is confidential for a five year period only.

ANSWER: *C*

16.   _____ means that the investigator explains the general purposes of the research and answers any questions of the subject at the end of the experiment.
        a.   Informed consent
        b.   Debriefing
        c.   Freedom to withdraw
        d.   Confidentiality

ANSWER: *B*

True-False

17.   The ethical investigator respects the participant's right to decline to serve in the research or to withdraw at any time, as long as the experiment does not suffer.

ANSWER: *F*

18.   Debriefing subjects and giving them a contact phone number and an address may not be sufficient in a high-risk study.

ANSWER: *T*

19.   Debriefing means that the investigator sends the final results of the study to each subject.

ANSWER: *F*

20.   In a simple perception experiment, in which the colour of symbols is the independent variable, little more than a general description of the experiment during the debriefing is probably required.

ANSWER: *T*

21.   The APA has provided special guidelines for psychologists on the use of drugs in research.

ANSWER: *T*

22.   The double-edged potentiality of scientific knowledge poses ethical problems only for psychologists.

ANSWER: *F*

23.   Most universities and research institutions have peer committees that judge the ethicality of proposed research.

ANSWER: *T*

24.   Once a study is approved by the appropriate agencies and committees, the investigator's responsibility for ensuring ethical treatment of participants is minimized.

ANSWER: *F*

25.   By providing enough information for informed consent, the research may undermine the validity of the experimental design.

ANSWER: *T*

Essay

26.   Describe the ethical issues that an investigator should consider when designing a study that induces a feeling of despair in its participants.

27.   Outline six of the ten APA general principles governing the conduct of research with human participants.

28.   What is speciesism? Outline an argument for and against speciesism.

** Text Page References for Test Questions can be found in Appendix C

How to Read and Write Research Reports

Key Terms

abstract	method
APA format	procedure
apparatus	references
author	report contents
checklist for critical readers	results
discussion	running head
failure	subjects
figures	tables
introduction	title

Lecture Suggestion

The instructor might wish to give the students some further experience in critically reading and evaluating journal articles by assigning students several short journal articles to read. The students should read the articles carefully and answer the Questions for Critical Readers presented in the text in Table 4-1.

These questions could then be discussed in class. Elmes (1978) presents a number of journal articles from various areas of psychology, many of which would be suitable for this exercise. In addition, several journal articles that would be good articles for this exercise are listed in the following Reference section.

References

Barefoot, J.C., Hoople, H., & McClay, D. (1972). Avoidance of an act which would violate personal space. Psychonomic Science, 28, 205-206.

Elmes, D.G. (1978). Readings in Experimental Psychology. Chicago: Rand McNally Publishing Company.

Frost, R., Katz, L., & Bentin, S. (1987). Strategies for visual word recognition and orthographical depth: A multilingual comparison. Journal of Experimental Psychology: Human Perception and Performance, 13, 104-115.

Hintzman, D.L., Carre, F.A., Eskridge, V.L., Owens, A.M., Shaff, S.S., & Sparks, M.E. (1972). Stroop effect: Input or output phenomenon. Journal of Experimental Psychology, 95, 458-459.

Roediger, H.L. & Crowder, R.G. (1972). Instructed forgetting: Rehearsal control or retrieval inhibition (repression)? Cognitive Psychology, 3, 244-254.

Roediger, H.L. & Payne, D.G. (1982). Hypermnesia: The role of repeated testing. Journal of Experimental Psychology: Learning, Memory, and Cognition, 8, 66-72.

Questions

Multiple Choice

1. At the beginning of the "Introduction" section is
   a. the heading "Introduction".
   b. the title.
   c. a brief summary of new findings.
   d. both a and b

ANSWER: *B*

2.   In a manuscript or report, you should
      a.   indicate where the tables should be placed in the "Discussion" section.
      b.   place tables on the same page.
      c.   number each table consecutively.
      d.   none of the above

ANSWER: *C*

3.   A journal article title should be
      a.   long, describing the variables and the most significant result
      b.   short, but giving some idea of the contents of the article
      c.   catchy or clever to arouse the reader's curiosity
      d.   humorous, if the article is boring

ANSWER: *B*

4.   The abstract of a journal article should
      a.   confuse the reader so that the reader will be forced to read on
      b.   be a lengthy summary of the article
      c.   be a short paragraph that summarizes the key points of the article
      d.   describe the theoretical considerations of the article for sophisticated readers who already know the research area

ANSWER: *C*

5.   The careful writer of an article or report avoids language that is
      a.   sexist.
      b.   ambiguous.
      c.   redundant.
      d.   all of the above

ANSWER: *D*

6.   The experienced researcher, in order to decide whether or not to read an entire journal article, will first read
      a.   the title and the abstract
      b.   the abstract and the introduction
      c.   the abstract and the results
      d.   the abstract and the references

ANSWER: *D*

7.   For an experienced researcher, a journal article will lose points when the references
      a.   follow the discussion section
      b.   are in alphabetical order rather than listed by year of publication
      c.   are not recent
      d.   all of the above

ANSWER: *C*

8.   Which of the following should be included in the "Introduction" of a journal article?
        a.   the predicted results
        b.   the obtained results
        c.   the hypothesis to be tested
        d.   the experimental design

ANSWER: *C*

9.   The "Method" section of a journal article should contain enough information for
        a.   another experimenter to replicate the study
        b.   the reader to have a general understanding of how the study was done
        c.   the reader to have a vague idea of how the study was done
        d.   the author to be able to remember what he did in case someone asks him

ANSWER: *A*

10.   Which of the following should not be included in the "Method" section of a journal article?
        a.   how the subjects were selected
        b.   the instructions given to human subjects
        c.   statistical design features
        d.   none of the above

ANSWER: *D*

11.   In general, use the past tense
        a.   in the review of other studies in your introduction.
        b.   in your method.
        c.   when describing and discussing your data.
        d.   both a and b

ANSWER: *D*

12.   Which of the following would you be unlikely to find in the "Results" section of a journal article?
        a.   graphs
        b.   summary tables
        c.   inferential statistics
        d.   raw data

ANSWER: *D*

13.   In the "Results" section of a journal article, inferential statistics are presented to
        a.   summarize the data
        b.   enable the reader to decide whether or not the data are reliable
        c.   enable the reader to decide whether or not the data are important and meaningful
        d.   enable the author to demonstrate that his results actually tested the hypothesis

ANSWER: *B*

14.   Inferential statistics about the data appear in statements like "$F(4,60) = 15.10, p < .01$." This means that if the experiment was done 100 times, the results would be similar in at least _____ of the cases.
        a.   90
        b.   95
        c.   99
        d.   100

ANSWER: *C*

15.   In reading the "Results" section of a journal article, you encounter the following statement: "Although the data just failed to reach the .05 level of significance, it is clear that the results are in the predicted direction." Which of the following remarks would the authors of your text make about the above statement?
        a.   It is acceptable to treat nonsignificant results as significant as long as the level of significance is stated.
        b.   Data should never be discussed if it is not statistically significant.
        c.   It is all right to discuss nonsignificant results as long as the results are in the predicted direction, otherwise they should not be discussed.
        d.   none of the above

ANSWER: *D*

16.   The appropriate level of significance for the statistical analysis of a given experiment is determined by
        a.   the situation
        b.   statistical convention
        c.   the journal editor
        d.   a fixed rule

ANSWER: *A*

17.   Which section of a journal article should the reader approach with the most scepticism?
        a.   Introduction
        b.   Discussion
        c.   Results
        d.   Method

ANSWER: *B*

18.   If you wanted to know what variables were used in an experiment, which section of the journal article would you read?
        a.   Method
        b.   Results
        c.   Introduction
        d.   Discussion

ANSWER: *A*

19.   The subject section tells the read
        a.   how many subjects were used.
        b.   how they were selected.
        c.   who they were.
        d.   all of the above

ANSWER: *D*

20.   The "Method" section of a journal article should include
        a.   considerations concerning subjects
        b.   a description of the apparatus used in the experiment
        c.   the procedure of the experiment
        d.   all of the above

ANSWER: *D*

21.   The dependent and independent variables are identified and described in the
        a.   Results
        b.   Introduction
        c.   Method
        d.   Abstract

ANSWER: *C*

22.   A lab report or journal article usually contains headings for all of the major sections of the paper
        except the:
        a.   Abstract
        b.   Introduction
        c.   Method
        d.   Results

ANSWER: *B*

23.   The most common type of title refers only to the
        a.   control and dependent variables
        b.   first line of the abstract
        c.   dependent and independent variables
        d.   most important conclusion of the article

ANSWER: *C*

24.   The abstract is a short paragraph usually containing about
        a.   25-50 words.
        b.   100-150 words.
        c.   200-300 words.
        d.   500 words.

ANSWER: *B*

25.   In the introduction, the author's review of the literature should include
        a.   only the most recent article related to the topic
        b.   all of the literature in any way related to the topic
        c.   the literature most relevant to the topic
        d.   only the literature published by the author

ANSWER: *C*

26.   In your research report, the cover page should include
        a.   the title
        b.   your name
        c.   your affiliation
        d.   all of the above

ANSWER: *D*

27.   The running head
        a.   appears at the top and centre of the page
        b.   appears at the top right-hand corner of the page
        c.   is a short title
        d.   both b and c

ANSWER: *D*

28.   The heading that appears at the top of each page of a manuscript or published article is
        a.   called the running head.
        b.   typed in capital letters near the bottom of the cover page of the copy manuscript.
        c.   excluded from the title page.
        d.   both a and b

ANSWER: *D*

True-False

29.   The method section may include an apparatus subsection.

ANSWER: *T*

30.   After reading the "Introduction" of a journal article, the key question concerns the author's goal.

ANSWER: *T*

31.   Because there are so many psychology articles published each month, journal article titles should be catchy or clever to catch a reader's attention.

ANSWER: *F*

32.   The abstract of a journal article is a short paragraph that summarizes the key points of an article.

ANSWER: *T*

33.   The Introduction of a journal article specifies the independent, dependent, and control variables used in the experiment.

ANSWER: *F*

34.   The importance of the experimental findings is usually discussed in the "Results" section.

ANSWER: *F*

35.   There is a fixed rule for setting an appropriate level of statistical significance.

ANSWER: *F*

36.   Captions for your figures are numbered consecutively and appear as a single page following the data tables.

ANSWER: *F*

37.   It is helpful to draw graphs from the data presented in tables.

ANSWER: *T*

38.   The way a graph or figure is drawn can emphasize or conceal obtained results.

ANSWER: *T*

39.   In a manuscript or journal article, the running head does not occur in the title page.

ANSWER: *F*

40.   Science is a social enterprise and if an author wants other scientists to read his journal articles then he or she should use common everyday language that the reader will understand.

ANSWER: *F*

41.   The discussion of a journal article is the most creative part of an article.

ANSWER: *T*

42.   Tables and figures must be used to describe and summarize data in an article published in a psychology journal.

ANSWER: *F*

43.   The past tense should be used in the review of other studies in the introduction and in the method section.

ANSWER: *T*

44.   Titles and journal names of referenced articles are abbreviated in psychology journals.

ANSWER: *F*

45.   The table of contents is a first step to selecting those articles in a journal relevant to your interests.

ANSWER: *T*

Essay

46.   State the questions that a critical reader should answer after reading each section of a journal article.

47.   An experimenter found that subjects recalled 52% of studied words and 58% of studied pictures. Graph the results in two ways, illustrating how a graph can emphasize or conceal a particular pattern of results. Which graph is more appropriate? Why? Label the graphs correctly.

48.   List the sections of a research report and describe the information contained in each section.

49.   Assume you are an editor of a journal. What criterion would you use in deciding whether to accept a particular paper?

50.   In reading the "Results" section of a journal article, you encounter the following statement: "Although the data just failed to reach the .05 level of significance, it is clear the results are in the predicted direction." Is this statement acceptable in an article? Why? How do you interpret that statement?

** Text Page References for Test Questions can be found in Appendix C

Psychophysics

Chapter Outline

Key Terms

absolute threshold	method of limits
beta (ß)	noise
criterion	nominal scale
d'	operational definition
decision threshold	ordinal scale
difference threshold	placebo
direct scaling	point of subjective equality
dolorimeter	psychophysical methods
false alarm	psychophysics
Fechner's law ($\Psi = k \log (S)$)	ratio scale
hit	receiver-operating
indirect scaling	characteristic (ROC)
interval of uncertainty	small-n designs
interval scale	staircase method
just-noticeable difference (JND)	Stevens' law ($\Psi = k S^n$)
magnitude estimation	theory of signal detection
measurement	threshold
measurement scales	Weber's law ($\Delta I/I = k$)

Answers to Discussion Questions

1. *The many practical uses of the method of limits in the determination of sensory thresholds are usually attributable to the ease and simplicity of this method, relative to the theory of signal detection. The practical uses of the method of limits is particularly evident in the design and marketing of consumer products. In the manufacture of stereo equipment, for example, the method of limits may be used to determine the minimum changes that are necessary in a system to produce a perceived difference in the customer. Such practical applications of the method are applied to many consumer products, from automobiles to cereals. The method of limits is also used in assessing and improving the design of equipment and other materials used by man.*

2. *As long as the procedures used when employing the method of limits and the staircase method are communicated (e.g., in the Method section of a journal article) with enough precision so that another researcher could replicate the procedure, then the two methods are equally "good" operational definitions of the concept of a threshold. The staircase method is a more efficient method, but this does not necessarily make it a better operational definition. An important point to be noted here is that the two methods might possibly lead to different estimates of a threshold, but as long as the operational definition of the threshold is the method by which the threshold was arrived at, there is no problem.*

3.

HIT RATE	FALSE ALARM RATE	d'
.90	.10	2.56
.90	.25	1.96
.90	.50	1.28
.90	.90	0

4. *An absolute threshold separates the stimulus dimension into detectable and undetectable components at a magnitude assumed to reflect the observer's sensitivity to that dimension. In contrast, a decision or response threshold supposes that an observer's sensory sensitivity of a stimulus dimension is a continuous distribution, and that the magnitude of detectibility varies according to the observer's sensory sensitivity to the stimulus dimension and the observer's criterion.*

5. *Ratio scale:　　　Weight of an object Speed of an automobile Interval scale: Fahrenheit and Centigrade IQ*
    Ordinal scale:　　10 most attractive people in a class Order in which race horses cross the finish line
    Nominal Scale:　　Student Identification Numbers on a football jersey

6. *Experiments using large numbers of subjects and inferential statistics such as analysis of variance typically do not exert precise control over the experimental setting. In this type of research statistical control helps make up for the lack of experimental control. In a small-n research project utilizing the same subjects across many observations or trials there is generally a large degree of experimental control. As a result, inferential statistics are seldom needed, although other statistics such as parameter estimates are often used. In all research there is a tradeoff between the degree of experimental control and the need for statistical control.*

Lecture Suggestion

Signal detection theory has had a major impact on many diverse areas of experimental psychology. The theory has also been applied in a wide variety of applied settings, including the analysis and evaluation of information-retrieval systems, inspection and quality control in various industrial settings (Drury, 1975), sonar target detection (Colguhoun, 1967) and many vigilance tasks (cf. Swets & Kristofferson, 1970). (Note, however, that there are limitations on the practical applicability of signal detection analysis - see Long and Waag, 1981, for a discussion of these limitations.) It would be instructive to present a practical problem to the class and see if the class could devise an experiment, using signal detection theory, to assess the sensitivity and response biases of observers in these "real world" conditions.

One interesting situation in which a signal detection analysis could be applied is in reading X-Rays of tumors. There are two types of "trials" - benign tumors and malignant tumors, and there are two types of response - "benign" and malignant. One way to do a signal detection experiment would be to use X-Ray films in which there were actually benign and malignant tumors. These could be presented to observers and the observers task would be to decide if the tumor was benign or malignant. Several interesting comparisons could made between different groups of subjects, such as first year medical students, interns, nurses, surgeons, etc. Also, an interesting issue is that of response criterion - how liberal or conservative should a surgeon be in making these decisions?

References

Colguhoun, W. P. (1967). Sonar detection as a decision process. Journal of Applied Psychology, 51, 187-190.

Drury, C. F. (1975). The inspection of sheet materials - Model and data. Human Factors, 17, 257-265.

Long, G. M. & Waag, W. L. (1981). Limitations on the practical applicability of d and measures. Human Factors, 23, 285-290.

Swets, J. A. & Kristofferson, A. B. (1970). Attention. Annual Review of Psychology, 21, 339-366.

Demonstration

It is a relatively easy matter to demonstrate that there is not a one-to-correspondence between the physical changes of a stimulus and our perception of these changes. Obtain a light source or sound generator which will allow the intensity of the stimulus to be varied. Present a stimulus of moderate intensity (the standard stimulus) and assign an arbitrary value to it (e.g., 100). Then present a comparison stimulus and ask the class to estimate how close the comparison stimulus is to the standard stimulus. The students should write down a number that represents the intensity of the comparison stimulus relative to the standard stimulus (the method of magnitude estimation). The instructor should record the value of the physical intensity of the comparison stimulus. Do this for several trials, varying the physical intensity of the comparison stimulus across a wide range. Using the mean of the students' responses, compare the values of the physical intensities with the perceived intensities. When data is collected in this way, the equation relating psychological value to physical value should be exponential:

$$Y = k \, (\text{stimulus})^n$$

It would also be interesting to note the variability of the students' responses, which would illustrate one of the reasons why psychophysical research employs small n designs.

Experimental Dilemma

1. A researcher interested in psychoaccoustics was using a very small number of subjects, or observers. Most of the observers were producing very stable performance measures, but one of the observers seemed to be rather erratic in his behavior. These observers were being paid for their services, so the researcher decided to see if the reason for this observers' erratic behavior was a shift in response criterion across experimental sessions. He decided to manipulate the observers criterion by changing the amount of money the observer was paid for each hit and each false alarm.

    On different days of this "mini-experiment" the observer was paid according to Schedule A and on the remaining days he was paid according to Schedule B (see below). These different schedules were counterbalanced across days using an appropriate counterbalancing scheme. For each schedule, depending upon the type of trial (Signal or Noise) and the observer's response, he either gained (+) or lost (-) the amount of money indicated.

	Schedule A				Schedule B	
	Signal	Noise			Signal	Noise
Yes	+1¢	-1¢		Yes	+5¢	-5¢
No	-1¢	+1¢		No	-5¢	+5¢

The results of the experiment showed that exactly the same results were obtained under Schedule A and Schedule B. That is, subjects produced exactly the same Hit and False Alarm rates under both schedules. Thus the d' values and the criterion was the same under the two payoff schedules.

The researcher concluded that the reason why the payoff schedules had no effect was that the manipulation of the payoff schedule was not extreme enough. In the next experiment the researcher planned to use 1¢ and 10¢ payoff schedules.

Do you agree with the researchers interpretation of the results? Why or why not? What results would you predict for the proposed experiment using 1¢ and 10¢ payoffs?

ANSWER: *This conclusion is wrong because the researcher failed to manipulate the relative cost of hits and false alarms. Both schedules are symmetric, and incorrect responses (False Alarms and Misses) would tend to make the observer set his criterion the same in the two conditions. In order to shift the subjects' criterion it is necessary to make the relative values of hits and false alarms different, say by making a hit worth 10¢ and a false alarm worth only 1¢, or vice versa.*

The researchers proposed experiment would not effectively change the subjects' criterion since, again, the payoff schedule would exhibit the same relative values for each type of outcome.

2.   A psychologist interested in the effect of personality traits upon various psychological abilities decided to test whether introverts or extraverts are more sensitive to external stimulation. His hypothesis was that introverts, who are basically quiet, shy people, would be more sensitive to the external world than would extraverts, who he thought would be more sensitive to internal stimulation. To test this hypothesis he decided to see which group of subjects would be better able to detect a vary faint amount of pressure applied to the back of the hand.

Ten introverts and 10 extraverts were selected on the basis of a personality test. All subjects were paid for their participation. Subjects were each tested individually by the same experimenter. Subjects were blindfolded and then given 200 trials. On half of the trials a very faint amount of pressure was applied to the back of the subjects hand by means of a mechanical device. The amount of pressure was constant for all subjects. On the remaining trials no pressure was applied to the subjects hand. All subjects were right handed, and only the right hand was used in the experiment. Finally, a different random order of pressure trials and no pressure trials was used for each subject. Subjects were not told how many trials there would be, only that there would be "a lot". No subject was told what percentage of trials would be "touch" trials.

Results showed that, averaged across subjects, the extraverts responded correctly on 85% of the touch trials and were incorrect on 15% of these trials. Introverts, however were only correct on 70% of the touch trials, making 30% errors on these trials. These differences between groups were reliable.

The researcher concluded that these results indicated that extraverts were more sensitive than introverts, since they were correct on more of the touch trials (85% versus 70%). Since this was exactly the opposite of what he had predicted, he decided that his hypothesis needed to be revised. Do you agree with this conclusion? Why or why not?

ANSWER: *Disagree, at least based on the data provided. We need to know what the false alarm rates were for these two conditions. A false alarm would be responding "touch" when no pressure was applied. Without the false alarm rates it is impossible to determine which group was more sensitive. What if the false alarm rate for the extraverts was 50% but for the introverts it was only 1%? What would the conclusion be then?*

Questions

Multiple Choice

1.   If a rock band turned up its amplifiers to produce twice as much energy as it produced before, the listener would experience a sound
    a.   twice as loud as before.
    b.   four times as loud as before.
    c.   one-half as loud as before.
    d.   none of the above

ANSWER: *D*

2.   Psychophysical methods can be used to measure judgments about
        a.   loudness
        b.   sweetness
        c.   happiness
        d.   both a and b

ANSWER: *D*

3.   The method of limits can be used to determine
        a.   an absolute threshold
        b.   a difference threshold
        c.   a response threshold
        d.   a decision threshold

ANSWER: *A*

4.   In general, the magnitude of the difference threshold _____ with _____ in the
        magnitude of the standard stimulus.
        a.   increases; decreases
        b.   decreases; increases
        c.   increases; increases
        d.   decreases; decreases
        e.   both c and d

ANSWER: *E*

5.   Who formalized the psychophysical methods?
        a.   Edward Boring
        b.   Gustav Fechner
        c.   Hermann Ebbinghaus
        d.   S.S. Stevens

ANSWER: *B*

6.   You are asked to decide if sugar is present in a cup of coffee? This is an example of a (an)
        a.   relative judgment
        b.   absolute judgment
        c.   response judgment
        d.   uncertainty judgment

ANSWER: *B*

7.   The most important control variable in a psychophysics experiment is
        a.   the stimulus magnitude
        b.   the stimulus duration
        c.   the subject's criterion
        d.   the subject's ability

ANSWER: *C*

8.   The physical correlate of the pitch of a tone is the _____ of the soundwave associated
        with that tone.
        a.   magnitude or amplitude
        b.   frequency
        c.   intensity
        d.   interval

ANSWER: *B*

9.   Pain judgements in response to increases in electrical intensity of shocks to the skin grow
        _____ loudness judgments in response to increases in sound energy.
        a.   much less rapidly than
        b.   less rapidly than
        c.   at about the same rate
        d.   much more rapidly than

ANSWER: *D*

10.   Which of the following is <u>not</u> an example of an operational definition?
        a.   great granddad's recipe for moonshine
        b.   an actor has memorized his lines when he can repeat all of his lines twice without an error
        c.   reaction time is the interval between the presentation of a stimulus and the subject's response
        d.   a rat is hungry when the rat craves food

ANSWER: *D*

11.   An ideal threshold would be a value of stimulus intensity such that stimulus intensities
        a.   above this threshold would always be detected
        b.   below this threshold would never be detected
        c.   equal to this threshold would never be detected
        d.   both a and b

ANSWER: *D*

12.   In actual practice, the threshold is operationally defined as the _____ of the points in
        each trial block where the observer switches from Yes to No (or No to Yes).
        a.   mean
        b.   median
        c.   mode
        d.   range

ANSWER: *A*

13.   A threshold based upon relative judgments where a constant comparison stimulus is judged relative to a series of changing stimuli is called the
    a.   mean threshold
    b.   absolute threshold
    c.   difference threshold
    d.   median threshold

ANSWER: C

14.   In a task where the observer compares the weight of a constant comparison stimulus with the weights of changing stimulus using the method of limits, the interval of uncertainty is operationally defined as
    a.   the mean of the upper and lower thresholds
    b.   the difference between the upper and lower thresholds
    c.   the distance between the means of the signal and noise distributions
    d.   the mean of the stimulus values corresponding to the last "heavier" response and the first "equal" response

ANSWER: B

15.   What is the threshold for the following set of data obtained using the staircase method?

		↓				Responses
	145	Yes				
	130	Yes	Yes	↓		Yes
Intensities	115	Yes	No	No		↑
	100	Yes	No			
	85	Yes	No			
	70	No	↑			
	55					

    a.   100
    b.   109
    c.   112.5
    d.   122.5

ANSWER: C

16.   In signal detection theory, moving the criterion to the left will
    a.   increase the hit rate
    b.   decrease the false alarm rate
    c.   decrease the miss rate
    d.   a and c

ANSWER: D

17. In signal detection theory, a liberal decision policy means the criterion will be set to the _____, and a conservative decision policy means the criterion will be set to the _____.
    a. left; right
    b. right; left
    c. right; right
    d. left; left

ANSWER: *A*

18. In a Receiver Operating Characteristic (ROC) function,
    a. d' is plotted as a function of the criterion (beta)
    b. hits are plotted as a function of false alarms
    c. hits are plotted as a function of d'
    d. false alarms are plotted as a function of the criterion (beta)

ANSWER: *B*

19. Boring, a history of psychology, claims that the introduction of psychophysics mark the onset of
    a. science.
    b. physics.
    c. scientific psychology.
    d. psychology.

ANSWER: *C*

20. In signal detection theory, the position of the criterion is determined by
    a. the decision process
    b. the sensory process
    c. the stimulus intensity
    d. the mean of the signal distribution

ANSWER: *D*

21. According to the theory of signal detection, perceptual judgments involve
    a. decision processes
    b. an absolute threshold
    c. sensory processes
    d. both a and c

ANSWER: *D*

Questions 22-24 are based on the Receiver Operating Characteristic function (ROC function) presented below.

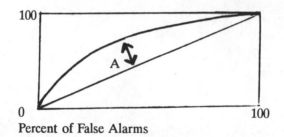

Percent of Hits

Percent of False Alarms

22.   In the above figure, the value of A corresponds to
       a.   the hit rate
       b.   the false alarm rate
       c.   the criterion (beta)
       d.   d'

ANSWER: *D*

23.   In the above figure, the diagonal line represents

       a.   chance performance
       b.   perfect performance
       c.   d'
       d.   the criterion (beta)

ANSWER: *A*

24.   In the above figure, the criterion can be determined from
       a.   the value of A
       b.   the diagonal
       c.   the slope of the ROC function
       d.   none of the above

ANSWER: *C*

25.   You decide that sugar is present in a cup of coffee in which there is no sugar. This is a
       a.   miss
       b.   hit
       c.   false alarm
       d.   correct rejection

ANSWER: *C*

26. The amount of overlap of the noise distribution and the signal-plus-noise distribution is determined by
    a. the strength of the signal
    b. the sensory sensitivity of the observer
    c. the interval of uncertainty
    d. both a and b

ANSWER: *D*

27. Subject are asked if sugar is present in a cup of coffee. Increasing the amount of sugar in the coffee will
    a. decrease d'
    b. increases d'
    c. have no affect on d'
    d. have an unpredictable affect on d'

ANSWER: *A*

28. At a horse race, the finishing positions are determined by how fast each horse ran the race. Thus, the first finishing horse ran the fastest, the second finishing horse ran the second fastest, and so on. These finishing position numbers from a(n) _____ scale.
    a. interval
    b. ratio
    c. ordinal
    d. nominal

ANSWER: *C*

29. Which of the following equations is called Fechner's Law?
    a. $Y = k \, (stimulus)^n$
    b. $Y = k \log (stimulus)$
    c. $Y = k \log (stimulus)^n$
    d. $Y = \log (stimulus)^n$

ANSWER: *B*

30. Which of the following equations is called Stevens' Power Law?
    a. $Y = \log (stimulus)^n$
    b. $Y = k \log (stimulus)$
    c. $Y = k \, (stimulus)^n$
    d. $Y = k \log (stimulus)^n$

ANSWER: *C*

31.   When a subject is asked to assign numbers to his or her observations, procedure is called
       a.   magnitude estimation
       b.   magnitude production
       c.   nominal scaling
       d.   interval estimation

ANSWER: *A*

32.   In psychophysical experiments, it is possible to generate to the ROC function by changing the subject's decision criterion from conservative to liberal. The experimenter can change the decision criterion by
       a.   changing the probability that a stimulus rather than noise only will be presented
       b.   changing the payoffs for hits and false alarms
       c.   increasing experimental control
       d.   both a and b

ANSWER: *D*

33.   In Weber's Law, the Weber fraction equals
       a.   the just noticeable difference
       b.   a constant
       c.   the difference threshold divided by the stimulus magnitude
       d.   all of the above

ANSWER: *B*

34.   When an observer compares the weight of a constant comparison stimulus with the weights of a changing stimulus using the method of limits, the point of subjective equality is operationally defined as
       a.   the mean of the stimulus values corresponding to the last "equal" response and the first "lighter" response
       b.   the mean of the stimulus values corresponding to the last "heavier" response and the first "equal" response
       c.   the difference between the upper and lower thresholds
       d.   the mean of a and b above

ANSWER: *D*

35.   In signal detection theory, the criterion determines
       a.   the hit rate
       b.   the false alarm rate
       c.   the miss rate
       d.   all of the above

ANSWER: *D*

36.   The scale of measurement that has the least stringent requirements is the _____ scale.
        a.   interval
        b.   ratio
        c.   ordinal
        d.   nominal

ANSWER: *D*

37.   Psychophysics involves the determination of the _____ reaction to events that lie along a _____ dimension.
        a.   physical; physical
        b.   physical; psychological
        c.   psychological; physical
        d.   psychological; psychological

ANSWER: *C*

True-False

38.   Measurement scales refer to the degree of precision with which we can assign numbers to objects.

ANSWER: *T*

39.   The psychophysical relation between stimulus and judgment depends on the particular sensory modality that is stimulated.

ANSWER: *T*

40.   The main thing that is controlled in a psychophysical experiment is the observer's strategy or frame of mind about his or her judgment.

ANSWER: *T*

41.   Using the method of limits, the alternating blocks of increasing and decreasing trials must each start at the same intensity.

ANSWER: *F*

42.   The mean of an upper and lower threshold is called the interval of uncertainty.

ANSWER: *F*

43.   Scientists using psychophysical techniques were able to formulate the first mathematical laws of psychological phenomena.

ANSWER: *T*

44.   The version of the method of limits called the staircase method is efficient because it concentrates responses around the threshold.

ANSWER: *F*

45.   Signal-detection theory assumes that noise is always present when a human attempts to detect signals.

ANSWER: *T*

46.   According to signal detection theory, whether an observer responds Yes or No depends upon the sensory impression and the decision criterion.

ANSWER: *T*

47.   An interval scale is changed if scale values are multiped by a constant.

ANSWER: *F*

48.   An absolute threshold is concerned with judgments about a single stimulus.

ANSWER: *T*

49.   An ordinal scale is changed if scale values are multiplied by a constant.

ANSWER: *F*

50.   Signal detection theory defines threshold in terms of the observer's decision criterion.

ANSWER: *F*

51.   The method of magnitude estimation requires the observer to detect which of two stimuli has the greater intensity, without regard to the degree of difference between the two stimulus intensities.

ANSWER: *F*

52.   A difference threshold is derived from judgments about a single stimulus.

ANSWER: *F*

53.   Steven's Power Law is based on an indirect scaling technique in which the observer responds in psychological units.

ANSWER: *F*

Essay

54.   Draw hypothetical distributions of the sensory impression resulting from noise and signal-plus-noise. Establish a low criterion and indicate which areas correspond to hits, misses, false alarms, and correct rejections. On a second figure, do the same with a high criterion.

55.   Briefly describe the method of limits, and discuss the concept of absolute and relative threshold.

56.   Describe how signal-detection theory alters the concept of a threshold held by classical psychophysicists.

57.   Describe briefly the key concepts concerning signal detection theory. How does signal detection theory approach the notion of a threshold?

58.   Describe the classical psychophysicist's idea of threshold. Outline the methods used by classical psychophysicists to evaluate the value for the threshold.

59.   Compare and contrast the small-n designs used in psychophysical research with the large-n design used in most other areas of psychology. Why are inferential statistics needed in research using large-n designs but generally not in small-n designs?

60.   Elaborate on the following statement, providing specific examples that support the statement: Psychophysics involves the determination of the psychological reaction to events that lie along a physical dimension.

61.   List two examples for each of the four types of measurement scales. Justify your examples by describing their critical characteristics.

** Text Page References for Test Questions can be found in Appendix C

Perception

Chapter Outline

Key Terms

awareness
blindsight
bottom-up processing
conceptually-driven processing
converging operation
data-driven processing
direct perception
double dissociation of function
dynamic perimetry
empirical theory
hallucination
illusion
impossible figure
indirect perception
masking
objective threshold

nativistic theory
perception
perceptual defense
perspective
phenomenological experience
priming
scotoma
sensation
size constancy
Stroop effect
subjective threshold
tachistoscope
top-down processing
unconscious inferences
verbal report

Answers to Discussion Questions

1.   *The word-superiority effect refers to the finding that the threshold to identify a letter is lower when the letter appears in a word than when it is presented alone or in a string of letters that does not form a word. One would account for the word-superiority effect with the information presented in figure 7-11 by relying on the notion of indirect or top-down processing. Perception of a letter such as the "H" in figure 7-11 benefits from information about the word ("THE"). Conceptual information about the word contributes to the identification of individual letters in the word. In the case of a single letter, or a letter contained in a nonword, there is no benefit of top-down conceptual processing. Consequently, a single letter or a letter in a nonword takes longer to identify than a letter in a word.*

2.   *In blindsight, there is a dissociation between verbal awareness and perceptual capacity in the scotoma: Persons with blindsight deny the existence of objects in the scotoma and yet they are able to make much better than chance judgments (e.g., localization, detection and orientation judgments) about the same objects. In a similar way, a person may report that he is unable to feel any pain and yet be able to localize the source of pain. This ability to localize the pain suggests a sensory capacity for detecting the pain without awareness of the pain. The research on perception without awareness also relates to the phenomena mentioned above. A person is unable to report the meaning of a word, or at times the presence of a word, and yet the meaning of that word may have an influence on the person's response on a task such as the Stroop task. Each of these cases reflect some form of perception without awareness. Consequently, the two-threshold theory proposed by Cheesman and Merikle can be used to account for the dissociation between the feeling of pain and the ability to locate the source of the pain, in that the level of the pain is between the subjective and objective thresholds.*

3.   *Converging operations identifying the unitary concept of dimensional integrality include direct similarity scaling, free classification, the existence of dimensionality preferences and the effects of dimensional discriminability of these preferences. Evidence for separable dimensions is obtained in sorting tasks where sorting speed is unaffected when dimensions are used redundantly and orthogonally.*

4.   *The experiments proposed in the text to investigate the warm-cool color distance illusion all involve*

the manipulation of hue. It might be of interest to examine the effects of saturation on this perceptual illusion. Casual observation of art works reveals that highly saturated warm colors are used in foregrounds whereas less saturated cool colors are used to denote distance. Present two chips of different saturations to subjects and have them estimate which chip is farther away. You would want to test at least three saturation levels of both a warm and a cool color with all possible combinations of these saturation levels for each individual color. All stimuli will be presented the same distance from the subject and subjects will have the option of reporting that the stimuli are equidistant. If the proposed hypothesis is correct then low saturation colors should always be judged to be farther away than high saturation colors for a given hue.

5. *One of the oldest known illusions is the apparent enlargement of the moon when it is near the horizon as compared with its perceived size when it is in the zenith. Several hypotheses have been offered concerning the mechanics of the illusion. These include differences in eye elevation when viewing the moon in these two positions, differences in perceived distance between the horizon and the zenith, and perceptual differences produced by the presence of open space when the moon is viewed in the zenith. Thus far, no compelling evidence has been offered for any of these explanations.*

    Some have argued that drawings made on a two-dimensional surface may be perceived as either arrangements in a plane or as three-dimensional representations. When they are regarded in the latter fashion, the illusion created may disappear. Consider the figure drawn below. In the Poggendorf illusion, the diagonal lines do not seem continuous upon first viewing for most people. However, if the rectangle is perceived as standing erect, the illusion vanishes.

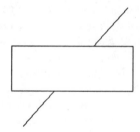

Lecture suggestion

In addition to the visual illusions discussed in the chapter, there are some visual illusions of movement that are well documented. That is, under the right circumstances, observers will report that a stimulus is moving from one point in the visual field to another when in actuality the stimulus remains fixed. The phi phenomenon occurs when two lights placed near one another in a dark visual field are lit in an alternating pattern. Observers perceive one light moving from one location to another rather than two lights being turned on and off (Wertheimer, 1912). This illusion of movement occurs for almost any two lights (or objects) as long as the physical distance between the two stimuli is small and the time interval between successive presentations is less than .03 seconds. As the time and distance intervals are increased it becomes more likely that the two stimuli will be perceived as distinct entities. The phi phenomenon is believed to occur because two different parts of the retina receive similar information in a short period of time. Since this is what occurs when an object actually moves across the visual field the event is perceived as the motion of one object rather than the presentation of two stationary objects.

Another interesting movement illusion is called the autokinetic phenomenon. If an observer fixates on a small light presented in an otherwise dark visual field, he or she will report that the light appears to move about erratically. This apparent movement probably results from satiation of the stimulated portion of the retina (Bruell & Albee, 1955). A real world instance of the autokinetic phenomenon was observed in pilots during World War II. Pilots monitoring tail lights of planes in front of them during night flights became disoriented when the tail lights began to "jump about". Today this problem is avoided by using flashing lights on planes instead of fixed lights.

References

Bruell, J.H. & Albee, G.W. (1955). Notes toward a motor theory of visual egocentric localization. Psychological Review, 62, 391-399.
Wertheimer, M. (1912). Experimentelle studien uber das sehen von bewegung. Zeit. Psychol., 61, 161-265.

Demonstration Suggestion

Since vision is the only sense modality discussed in the text, it might be useful to demonstrate the specialization of another type of perception, namely taste. Research has generally shown that the wide variety of tastes that we experience are merely combinations of four sensations-- sweetness, sourness, saltiness, and bitterness. The taste buds are the sense organs through which we derive our taste perceptions and they are located primarily on the front, back, and outer edges of the tongue. Certain areas of the tongue are more sensitive to particular tastes than others. For instance, taste buds on the tip of the tongue are responsible for out perception of sweetness and saltiness. The sides of the tongue respond most to sour tastes. Finally, the taste buds at the back of the tongue are most sensitive to bitter tastes. This degree of specialization may be easily demonstrated in the classroom setting. Use sugar, lemon juice, salt, and vinegar to elicit the four basic taste sensations. Apply these substances to different portions of the tongue using cotton swabs. It might be instructive to blindfold students and record accuracy as they try to guess particular tastes applied to portions of the tongue that are least sensitive to those tastes.

Experimental Dilemmas

1.   An experimenter wishes to examine the effects of context on the perception of auditory stimuli. Specifically, he wishes to investigate the probability of detecting low frequency tones in the presence of high frequency tones. The hypothesis is that subjects will be less likely to hear low frequency tones when they are presented amidst a preponderance of high frequency tones than when only low frequency tones are presented. Two groups of subjects will be tested. An experimental group will hear both low and high frequency tones presented at random intervals to the right ear. In order to enhance context effects, the experimenter plans to present the low frequency tones at 20 decibels of loudness and the high frequency tones at 60 decibels of loudness. Eighty percent of the stimuli will be high frequency tones and 20 percent will be low frequency tones. A control group will hear only low frequency tones all presented at 20 decibels at random intervals. All tones will be presented to the right ear. The task for subjects in both groups is simply to press a button whenever they hear a tone presented. Are there any problems with this experimental design or procedure? If so, what are they?

ANSWER: *One problem with the design is that the experimenter has not equated stimulus intensity across the two groups. If a difference in the probability of detecting low frequency tones is obtained between the two groups we could not be sure whether this difference is due to the presence of high frequency tones in the experimental group or to the fact that there are both high and low intensity stimuli in the experimental group. Thus, all tones should be presented at the same decibel level. In addition another control group should be tested in which high and low frequency tones are presented with equal probability. Data from such a group could be examined to insure us that any differences between detection of low and high frequency tones is due to context and not to the fact that high frequency tones are detected better than low frequency tones, or vice-versa.*

2.   An experimenter hypothesizes that low intensity visual stimuli are detected better in the periphery than in the center of the visual field. In order to test this hypothesis she presents faint flashes of light to different areas of the visual field in a random fashion. Each subject is placed in an apparatus that holds his or her head in place and is instructed to gaze directly ahead during the task. After being dark adapted for 20 minutes upon entering the laboratory, the visual stimuli are presented to the subject. The time intervals between stimuli and their places of occurrence in the visual field are randomized so that subjects cannot predict where or when the next stimulus will occur. Subjects are instructed to press a button whenever a stimulus is detected anywhere in the visual field. The experimenter plans to compare the number of detections of stimuli in the periphery with the number of detections in the center of the visual field. Are they any problems with this design or procedure? If so, what are they?

ANSWER: *There are no problems.*

Questions

Multiple Choice

1.   _____ are a set of two or more operations used to eliminate alternative explanations for a set of experimental results.
    a.   Top-down processes
    b.   Bottom-up processes
    c.   Diverging operations
    d.   Converging operations

ANSWER: *D*

2.   Psychologists study illusions because
    a.   illusions illustrate that perception is not always accurate.
    b.   illusions illustrate that perception is based on probabilities and not certainties.
    c.   subjects are seldom fooled by illusions.
    d.   both a and b

ANSWER: *D*

3.   The _____ view of perceptual processing emphasizes the role of sensory data in determining what is perceived.
   a.   top-down
   b.   bottom-up
   c.   converging operations
   d.   diverging operations

ANSWER: *B*

4.   Which of the following is used as a cue in depth perception?
   a.   relative size
   b.   haze
   c.   both a and b
   d.   neither a nor b

ANSWER: *C*

5.   Size constancy occurs when
   a.   depth cues are used to account for distance between an observer and an object being perceived.
   b.   an observer detects no difference in size between a large object presented against a dark background and a small object presented against a light background.
   c.   an object is perceived to be further away than another object due to overlap cues.
   d.   none of the above

ANSWER: *A*

6.   Which of the following is an example of size constancy?
   a.   You report that the book in front of your is larger than the one across the room because the image on your retina is larger for the closer book.
   b.   You report that the small dog at your feet is the same size as the larger dog down the street.
   c.   You correctly report that the lamp on the table beside you is the same size as the one you see further down the hall.
   d.   all of the above

ANSWER: *C*

7.   Closely related to the direct/indirect issue is
   a.   the relative and innate factors.
   b.   the distinction between bottom-up and top-down processing.
   c.   the role of converging operations in understanding perception.
   d.   both a and b

ANSWER: *D*

8.   Illusions that psychologists study in the laboratory
      a.   are artificially created and tell us little about perception in the real world.
      b.   help to illustrate components of everyday perception that are used inside and outside the laboratory.
      c.   help to highlight the reliability and accuracy of perceptual reports.
      d.   validate the use of phenomenological reports.

ANSWER: *B*

9.   The three levels of perceptual recognition in McClelland and Rumelhart's theory are
      a.   letter, word, sentence
      b.   feature, letter, word
      c.   geon, feature, letter
      d.   feature, word, schema

ANSWER: *B*

10.   The _____ of an auditory stimulus, is analogous to its pitch and the _____ of the stimulus refers to its loudness.
      a.   waveform; intensity
      b.   timbre; frequency
      c.   frequency; timbre
      d.   frequency; intensity

ANSWER: *D*

11.   In the McClelland and Rumelhart model of visual word recognition, the second level is the _____ level.
      a.   geon
      b.   feature
      c.   letter
      d.   word

ANSWER: *C*

12.   To be useful to a psychologist, a phenomenological report must be
      a.   reliable.
      b.   verifiable.
      c.   an introspective response.
      d.   verbal.

ANSWER: *B*

13.   Which of the following is true?
        a.   All reports are responses.
        b.   All responses are reports.
        c.   A response is a report if a relationship between the response and a perceptual event can be indirectly inferred.
        d.   A phenomenological report is of interest in and of itself but a response is not.

ANSWER: *A*

14.   We concluded that the pecking responses of pigeons observed by Blough (1958) qualified as reports because
        a.   a peck on one key indicated that food would be delivered.
        b.   knowing which key was pecked allowed an inference as to whether the pigeon could see the stimulus.
        c.   knowing which key was pecked provided no information as to whether the pigeon could see the stimulus.
        d.   pigeons pecked keys regardless of whether they saw a stimulus.

ANSWER: *B*

15.   A fundamental issue(s) concerning perception is
        a.   the nature/nurture controversy
        b.   the direct/indirect controversy
        c.   the importance of past experience and innate factors
        d.   both a and c

ANSWER: *D*

16.   Persons with blindsight are
        a.   aware of objects in the scotoma
        b.   are unaware of objects in all of their visual field
        c.   are unaware of objects in the scotoma
        d.   are aware of objects outside of the scotoma
        e.   both c and d

ANSWER: *E*

17.   In the McClelland and Rumerhart model of visual word recognition, word units
        a.   mutually inhibit each other.
        b.   mutually activate each other.
        c.   remain independent.
        d.   reactivate the features.

ANSWER: *A*

18. In establishing an objective threshold, which of the following tests is most appropriate?
   a. forced-choice recognition
   b. verbal reports
   c. localization judgments
   d. free recall

ANSWER: *A*

19. In his experiments, Marcel manipulated the observer's awareness of the priming word by presenting a jumbled pattern of letters _____ the onset of the priming word
   a. immediately before
   b. at the same time as
   c. immediately after
   d. long before

ANSWER: *C*

20. In the McClelland and Rumelhart model of visual word recognition, as soon as a word unit is activated by letters, then _____ are reactivated.
   a. the features
   b. the letters
   c. the features and letters
   d. the features, letters and word

ANSWER: *B*

21. The Stroop task
   a. involves naming the color of ink that a word is printed in.
   b. involves naming the color of an object as it would normally occur (e.g., saying "yellow" to "lemon").
   c. requires subjects to read words aloud as they are presented.
   d. requires subjects to read profane words aloud.

ANSWER: *A*

22. The Stroop effect
   a. occurs when colors are named slowly for words that match the color name.
   b. occurs when colors are named slowly for words that denote a color name other than the one being named.
   c. occurs when words are named slowly due to the color in which they are printed.
   d. occurs when words are named slowly due to their physical similarity with other words presented in the experiment.

ANSWER: *B*

23.   In Marcel's Stroop experiment, the difference between the aware and unaware trials was the time
        between the onset of the _____ and the _____.
        a.   prime word; color patch
        b.   mask; color patch
        c.   prime word; mask
        d.   prime word; target word

ANSWER: *C*

24.   In Cheesman and Merikles' experiment, the standard Stroop effect was found in which of the four
        conditions?
        a.   25%, 55%, 90%, and no mask
        b.   55%, 90% and no mask
        c.   90% and no mask
        d.   25%, 55% and 90%

ANSWER: *B*

25.   According to the two-threshold theory, below the _____ threshold people claim they are unaware
        of the stimulus, and above the _____ threshold their behavior is sensitive to the meaning of the
        stimulus.
        a.   subjective; subjective
        b.   objective; subjective
        c.   objective; objective
        d.   subjective; objective

ANSWER: *D*

26.   The most important reason for a psychologist to use converging operations is to
        a.   support inferences about processes that cannot be directly inferred.
        b.   replicate an experimental finding to insure its reliability.
        c.   increase precision of the dependent variable.
        d.   define a process in terms of its operations.

ANSWER: *A*

27.   Many illusions are created because our interpretation of the world does not correspond to external
        reality. However, when we know the true state of the external world
        a.   our perceptions are always correct.
        b.   our perceptions do not always improve.
        c.   we ignore the knowledge because our senses are always believed to be correct.
        d.   we ignore our perceptions and rely on our new-found knowledge.

ANSWER: *B*

28.   A phenomenological report
    a.   occurs when an observer describes his or her perceptual experience.
    b.   is useful only to the extent that it provides information about an event that the experimenter cannot observe directly.
    c.   cannot be directly verified by the experimenter.
    d.   all of the above

ANSWER: *D*

29.   The warm-cool color distance illusion refers to the fact that
    a.   artists use reds and yellows in the backgrounds of paintings to give the illusion of three dimensions.
    b.   blues and greens in the foreground of a picture denote three dimensions instead of two.
    c.   reddish colors appear to move toward the viewer whereas bluish hues appear to recede into the background.
    d.   colors are perceived as being warmer when presented near the viewer but are judged cooler when moved further away.

ANSWER: *C*

30.   Data-driven processing is to _____ processing as conceptually-driven processing is to _____.
    a.   bottom-up; top-down
    b.   top-down; bottom-up
    c.   indirect; direct
    d.   primary; secondary

ANSWER: *A*

True-False

31.   Perceptions are based upon probabilities rather than certainties.

ANSWER: *T*

32.   The evidence for perceptual capacity in the scotoma of blindsight persons is the ability to verbally report the presence of objects in the scotoma.

ANSWER: *T*

33.   Perceptual defense is localized in the perceptual system.

ANSWER: *F*

34.   Size constancy occurs when an object is judged to be a different size at different distances from the observer.

ANSWER: *F*

35.   Although we may be fooled by visual illusions at first, our perception will be improved once we obtain knowledge of how an illusion works.

ANSWER: *F*

36.   Although verbal report is one dependent variable used in perceptual research, psychologists prefer to use more objective measures such as reaction time.

ANSWER: *T*

37.   Converging operations provide the only way of arriving at an experimental conclusion.

ANSWER: *F*

38.   A report is interesting only to the extent that it verifies an observation made directly by the experimenter.

ANSWER: *F*

39.   The response of an observer qualifies as a report when a verifiable relationship between the response and a previous perceptual event can be directly inferred.

ANSWER: *T*

40.   Perception provides you with the elements necessary for sensation.

ANSWER: *F*

41.   Phenomenological reports are not analytic; they are attempts to describe whole experiences rather than attempts to isolate separate elements of experiences.

ANSWER: *T*

42.   Overt behaviors such as key presses are not as informative as verbal statements when used as reports.

ANSWER: *F*

43.   According to the indirect view of perception, we interpret a scene in order to produce a perception of depth and distance.

ANSWER: *T*

44.   Helmholtz proposed that all our knowledge of depth (and the rest of visual perception) was innate.

ANSWER: *F*

45.   Converging operations are a set of two or more operations that suggest alternative explanations for an experimental result.

ANSWER: *F*

46.   The general finding in the Stroop task is that the time required to name ink color decreases when the stimulus word is the name of a color other than the ink it is printed in.

ANSWER: *F*

47.   An experimenter can be satisfied that he or she has eliminated alternative explanations of an experimental result if two converging operations have led to the same conclusion.

ANSWER: *F*

48.   Masking involves presenting a jumbled pattern of letters after the priming word has been identified.

ANSWER: *F*

49.   Color is composed of three components-- hue, saturation, and brightness.

ANSWER: *T*

50.   Perceptual defense refers to the fact that profane words are reported more quickly in a pronunciation task than ordinary words.

ANSWER: *F*

Essay

51.   All reports are responses but not all responses are reports. What is the difference? Give an example of a phenomenological report and discuss why it is not considered a merely a response.

52.   Discuss how the direct/indirect issue parallels the distinction between bottom-up and top-down perceptual processing.

53.   Two important issues concerning perception are the direct/indirect controversy and the nature/nurture controversy. Describe each controversy and explain how they are similar and different.

54.   The word "YES" is presented visually to a person. Describe (with a schematic) the recognition process according to the McClelland and Rumelhart model of visual word recognition.

55.   Marcel used the Stroop procedure to examine perception without awareness. Describe the experimental procedures, the findings and the interpretation of the findings.

** Text Page References for Test Questions can be found in Appendix C

Attention and Reaction Time

Chapter Outline

Key Terms

additive factors	interstimulus interval
attention	monitoring
bit	overload
choice reaction	personal equation
confounding	reaction time
dichotic listening	recall delay
Donders A reaction	serial position
Donders B reaction	shadowing
Donders C reaction	simple reaction
error rate	speed-accuracy tradeoff
factors	subtractive method
interaction	transformation

Answers to Discussion Questions

1. *Kinnebrook could have argued that the reason why his crossing times were longer than those of his boss is that Kinnebrook's simple reaction time (i.e., his reaction time on a Donders' A reaction task) was greater than his boss. If there were a constant difference between Kinnebrook and his boss on such a simple reaction time task, then that difference could be subtracted from Kinnebrook's crossing times in order to make them comparable to his boss' crossing times.*

2. *One of the critical assumptions underlying the subtractive method is the assumption of pure insertion. That is, according to the subtractive method one creates two different tasks in which the reaction time can be measured, where the second task is believed to require all of the mental operations of the first, plus an additional operation. This assumption is inherent in the use of Donders' subtractive method (see Figure 8-4 in the text). The difference in the mean reaction time between a Donders' C reaction and a Donders' reaction is assumed to be an estimate of the inserted stage of stimulus identification. The assumption here is that adding, or inserting, this stimulus selection stage has no effect upon the other stages.*

    The additive factors method replaces the assumption of pure insertion with a weaker assumption, namely the assumption of selective influence. Instead of requiring that a change in the task result in the insertion or removal of an entire processing stage without affecting the other stages, the assumption of selective influence only requires that a change in the task influence the duration of some stage, without altering others. This difference in the assumed consequences of changing a task represents one major difference between the subtractive method and the additive factors method.

    Another critical difference between the additive factors method and the subtractive method concerns the duration of processing stages. Whereas the subtractive method provides a means by which to estimate the duration of a stage (e.g., Donders C reaction time minus Donders A reaction time provides an estimate of the time required for stimulus identification), the additive factors method provides no such method for estimating the duration of processing stages.

    Taylor (1976) discusses a number of problems associated with the additive factors method. First, the fact that two factors fail to interact does not necessarily mean that these two stages do not influence any stages in common. A second related problem is that there may be little correspondence between the stages of the mental processes and the stages of the theorists' model.

3. *This experiment confounds the order of the fast and slow presentation rates and the sex of the subject. That is, women receive the fast presentation rate first and then the slow rate, whereas the men receive the slow rate first and then the fast rate. One simple way to remove this confound is to make the rate of*

presentation a between-subjects factor, and give half of the men and half of the women the fast presentation rate and give the remaining subjects the slow presentation rate. An alternative solution is to give half of each group the slow rate followed by the fast rate, while the remaining half of the subjects receive the reverse order. This design would allow the researchers to determine whether there are any differential transfer effects for the slow and the fast presentation rates.

4.   (a) *At the grocery store you need to buy some fresh fruit. You can either go slow and make few errors (an error being the selection of a piece of 'bad' fruit) or go quickly and be more likely to make an error.*
(b) *Math homework can be done slowly and carefully or quickly with more errors being made.*
(c) *A person who does not type very well can type at a slow rate and make few errors, but if he is under time pressure he might type more quickly, but make more errors.*
(d) *When mail is sorted into mailboxes few errors will be made if the mail clerk works at a slow rate, but at a faster rate more errors might be expected to occur.*
(e) *A cashier is more likely to make an error in giving a customer her change when he is in a rush, as compared to when he is working at a normal rate. Situation (a) could be tested in a laboratory experiment by having a large box of fruit of various types. The subjects' task is to select a specified number of each type of fruit, and not select any damaged fruit. In several conditions subjects could be given different amounts of time to perform this task. A variable that might also be manipulated is the proportion of fruit that is "bad". This experiment would show the fewest errors when the subjects are given a lot of time, with more and more errors being made as the time limit is made shorter. This might interact with the proportion of bad fruit, with the greatest number of errors being made when there is a lot of bad fruit and there is not much time to select the fruit. Situation (b) could be tested by giving subjects sheets with math problems printed on them, and then telling different groups of subjects to try to finish all of the problems but within different time limits. Other factors that could be manipulated here are the math backgrounds of the subjects and the type and difficulty of the problems provided.*

Lecture Suggestion

The <u>Lecture Suggestion</u> for Chapter 3 presents a brief description of an experiment reported by Gray and Wedderburn (1960) that called into question the early selection aspect of Broadbent's (1958) filter model. In the present chapter the instructor can discuss several alternative models of selective attention. These models can be contrasted with Broadbent's model, and the evidence that supports these alternative models can be discussed. Appropriate models to discuss here would include Treisman's (1964) attenuation model, Deutsch and Deutsch's (1963) selective response model, and Norman's (1968) model or selective attention. (See Lachman, Lachman, and Butterfield, 1979; Norman, 1976).

References

Broadbent,   D.E. (1958). <u>Perception and Communication</u>. London: Pergamon Press.
Deutsch, J.A. & Deutsch, D. (1963). Attention: Some theoretical considerations. <u>Psychological Review, 70,</u> 80-90.
Lachman, R., Lachman, J. L., & Butterfield, E.C. (1979). <u>Cognitive psychology and information processing: An introduction</u>. Hillsdale, New Jersey: Lawrence Erlbaum Associates.
Norman, D.A. (1968). Toward a theory of memory and attention. <u>Psychological Review, 75,</u> 522-536.
Norman, D.A. (1976). <u>Memory and attention: An introduction to human information processing</u> (2 ed.). New York: Wiley.
Treisman, A.M. (1964). Verbal cues, language and meaning in selective attention. <u>American Journal of Psychology, 77,</u> 206-219.

Demonstration

Reaction time measures have been used in a wide variety of experimental settings. One very interesting example of using reaction time measures to infer mental processes is series of mental rotation experiments reported by Shepard and his colleagues (e.g., Cooper & Shepard, 1973; Shepard & Metzler, 1971). In these experiments subjects are shown either an "R" in normal orientation, or an "R" in backward orientation. When presented with these stimuli the subjects task is to decide whether the stimulus is in normal orientation or in the backward orientation. However, the stimulus items can also be rotated away from the upright orientation by various degrees of rotation. Cooper and Shepard (1973) showed that subjects judgment times increase as a function of the deviation of the stimulus item away from its normal upright orientation.

The Cooper and Shepard experiment can be modified as a classroom demonstration. The stimulus materials should be a series of 'R's in normal and reverse orientation, with some of the stimuli upright and some displaced by various angles of rotation to the right or left. The stimuli should be prepared as transparencies or as slides. Select one student to serve as the subject. Reaction time can be measured using a stopwatch. Measure the time from when the stimulus is presented until when the subject responds "normal" or "reverse". Also keep track of the number of errors.

After a number of trials has been run, compute the median reaction time for each angle of displacement. (Means of reaction times may give misleading results, since a mean can be greatly affected by one very long reaction time.) These medians can then be plotted as a function of the orientation of the stimulus. Do these data correspond to Cooper and Shepards' findings?

References

Cooper, L.A. & Shepard, R. N. (1973). Chronometric studies of the rotation of mental images. In W.G. Chase (Ed.), Visual Information Processing. New York: Academic Press.

Shepard, R.N. & Metzler, J. (1971). Mental rotation of three dimensional objects. Science, 171, 701-703.

Experimental Dilemmas

1. A traffic safety researcher was interested in the effect of the location of a visual stimulus upon reaction times. He had a hunch that the closer a visual stimulus was to the center of the visual field the faster the reaction time would be. He felt that if this were true then it would make more sense to place automobile brake lights in the center of the car than on the outside edges of the car. He tested this hypothesis by using a four choice reaction time task.

   The subjects were seated before a display of four small red lights. The two middle lights were close to the center of the visual field, while the two remaining lights were placed at a distance of 24 inches on either side of the two central lights. On each trial one of the four lights came on and the subjects' task was to press one of four response buttons. Each button corresponded to one of the four stimulus lights. Subjects were given 100 trials, 25 for each light and the order of presentation of the stimulus lights was randomly determined for each subject.

   The results for the experiment are as follows. Light number refers to the position of the light, with lights 1 and 4 being the "outside" lights and lights 2 and 3 being the "inside", or centrally located, lights.

Light Number	RT in msec	Error Rate
1	682	3.1%
2	607	4.3%
3	599	4.4%
4	687	3.0%

Statistical analysis revealed that the two outside lights produced reliably longer reaction times than did the two inside lights. Also, the two outside lights were not reliably different from one another, nor were the two inside lights.

The safety researcher concluded that these results support his hypothesis that centrally located visual stimuli will produce faster reaction times than will be peripherally located stimuli. Do you agree with this conclusion? Why or why not?

ANSWER: *Disagree. There is clear evidence of a speed accuracy tradeoff in these data, in that there is an inverse relation between reaction time and the error rate, with the condition with the shortest reaction time producing the highest error rate and the condition with the longest reaction time producing the lowest error rate.*

2.   In an experiment using a dichotic listening task there were two types of subjects and two rates of item presentation. The results of that experiment are given below.

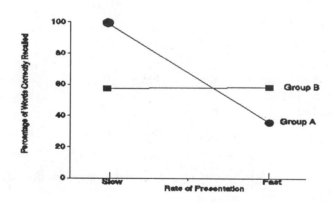

These results show a reliable interaction of the type of subject (A vs. B) x rate of presentation. Also, there was a reliable effect of group even for the slow presentation rate. The researcher published these results and argued that the reliable interaction provided support for his theory of personality type (i.e., type A persons versus type B persons).

After these data were published another researcher criticized the first researchers' conclusion. The second researcher argued that this interaction was caused by scale attenuation (i.e., a floor effect), and that without these floor effects there would not have been an interaction. The first researcher replied that his interaction could not be explained simply by scale attenuation.

Which researcher do you agree with and why?

ANSWER: *The first researcher is correct. Crossover interactions such as this one cannot be attributed to scale attenuation or to the scale used for the dependent variable.*

Questions

Multiple Choice

1. _____ is the item's location in an ordered list.
    a. Temporal position
    b. List position
    c. Serial position
    d. Stimulus discriminability

ANSWER: *C*

2. In an experiment, confounding occurs when
    a. more than one independent variable is manipulated
    b. an uncontrolled variable covaries with an independent variable
    c. an interaction occurs between two independent variables
    d. an interaction occurs between three or more independent variables

ANSWER: *B*

3. Confounding can occur
    a. only in small n designs
    b. only in experiments with one independent variable
    c. only in factorial experiments
    d. in any experimental design

ANSWER: *D*

4. In the Knight and Kantowitz (1974) experiment, recall delay is the time between presentation of an item within a dichotic pair and
    a. recall of the word.
    b. presentation of the probe word.
    c. presentation of the next item.
    d. recall of the probe word.

ANSWER: *B*

5.   Which of the following represents a Donders' A reaction?
    a.   A receptionists' telephone has several buttons corresponding to different telephone numbers.
            When the telephone rings the receptionist responds by pressing the button that is flashing on
            and off.
    b.   When a resident of the apartment building rings a bell the security guard responds by pressing
            a button that opens the front door. If a nonresident rings the bell the guard does not let that
            person in the building.
    c.   When a bicyclist sees a Stop sign he puts on his brakes to stop.
    d.   When the alarm clock goes off a person can either press the "snooze" button or else turn the
            alarm off.

ANSWER: *C*

6.   In an experiment an interaction can be obtained only when
    a.   the experiment involves more than one independent variable
    b.   the experiment involves more than one dependent variable
    c.   the experiment confounds either two independent variables or two psychological processes
    d.   the results depend upon the combination of the independent variables

ANSWER: *A*

7.   An experimenter obtained the following reaction times for three tasks:
            Task 1:   250 msec
            Task 2:   350 msec
            Task 3:   500 msec
        Donders' subtractive method predicts that Task 1 is the _____ task, Task 2 is the
        _____ task and task 3 is the _____ task.
    a.   A (simple) reaction; B (choice) reaction; C reaction
    b.   A reaction; C reaction; B reaction
    c.   B reaction; A reaction; C reaction
    d.   B reaction; C reaction; A reaction

ANSWER: *B*

8.   The following reaction times were obtained for one subject.
        Donders' A (simple) reaction task = 200 msec
        Donders' B (choice) reaction task = 350 msec
        Donders' C reaction task = 400 msec
        Based on these reaction times, using Donders' subtractive method for estimating the time required
        for mental operations, how long would you estimate the identification process tasks?
    a.   50 msec
    b.   200 msec
    c.   150 msec
    d.   using Donders' method the identification time cannot be computed from these data

ANSWER: *B*

9.   When using the additive factors method, experimental manipulations are used to
        a.   alter the number of stages involved in a task
        b.   alter the duration of stages
        c.   alter the error rates
        d.   change tasks from simple (A) reaction tasks into choice (B) reaction tasks

ANSWER: *B*

10.   _____ can be used as a dependent variable in an experiment examining attention.
        a.   Reaction time
        b.   Heart rate
        c.   Pupil diameter
        d.   all of the above

ANSWER: *D*

11.   According to the additive factors method, in order to discover how processing stages are related one needs to
        a.   look for patterns of interaction and additivity of reaction time
        b.   add the reaction times of the various simple tasks in order to estimate the overall reaction time for more complex tasks
        c.   compare the relation of the reaction time and the overall error rate
        d.   factorially combine within the same experiment Donders A, B, and C reactions

ANSWER: *A*

12.   The dependent measure "bits" is a measure of
        a.   information
        b.   stimulus intensity
        c.   stimulus duration
        d.   the time required by a processing stage

ANSWER: *A*

13.   In the dichotic listening task, two separate and independent messages are presented so that
        a.   each message is heard in each ear
        b.   both messages are heard in one ear and only one message is heard in the other ear
        c.   each message is heard in a different ear
        d.   both messages are heard in one ear and no message is heard in the other ear

ANSWER: *C*

14.   Biederman and Kaplan (1970) examined whether _____ and _____ influenced the same stages of mental processing.
        a.   stimulus discriminability; stimulus response compatibility
        b.   number of stimulus; stimulus discriminability
        c.   number of responses; stimulus response compatibility
        d.   number of stimulus; number of responses

ANSWER: *A*

15.   Operationally, confounding must always be traced back to
        a.   independent variables
        b.   control variables
        c.   uncontrolled variables
        d.   both a and c

ANSWER: *D*

16.   If an experiment contains a confound, then
        a.   it is impossible to interpret the results of the experiment
        b.   when the experiment is replicated with the confound removed the results will differ from those
                of the original experiment
        c.   the results are not replicable
        d.   it is important to evaluate statistically the reliability of the results

ANSWER: *A*

17.   The difference between a monitoring task and a shadowing task is that
        a.   the shadowing task allows the experimenter to be certain that attention has been devoted to
                the attended message
        b.   the shadowing task is more difficult than the monitoring task
        c.   the shadowing task requires the subject to repeat the attended message, whereas the
                monitoring task does not
        d.   both a and c

ANSWER: *D*

18.   In a dichotic listening experiment, if a researcher wants to be certain that her subject has devoted
        attention to at least one message, then she should
        a.   use a shadowing task
        b.   require her subject to repeat the attended message after the message is completed
        c.   use a monitoring task and present very distinct messages to the left and right ears
        d.   present the two messages in different voices

ANSWER: *A*

19.   In a dichotic listening experiment, the fact that subjects recall some information from the
        unattended message is important because
        a.   it suggests subjects were not paying attention to the attended message
        b.   it suggests that subjects can attend equally to two messages
        c.   it suggests unattended messages are processed to some degree
        d.   none of the above; when recall is this poor there is a floor effect

ANSWER: *C*

20.   Norman (1969) argued that in a typical shadowing experiment a subject could attend to the
       nonshadowing message as well as the shadowed message, but the poor recall of the nonshadowed
       message was due to memory loss resulting from prevention of rehearsal. Norman was thus arguing
       that
       a.   in typical shadowing experiments the shadowed versus nonshadowed manipulation was not
             effective enough to affect performance
       b.   the results of the previous shadowing experiments were not replicable
       c.   researchers should use a monitoring task instead of a shadowing task, since a monitoring task
             avoids the problem of identifying which message is to be attended
       d.   the previous shadowing experiments had confounded memory processes and attentional
             processes

ANSWER: *D*

21.   Knight and Kantowitz (1975) presented pairs of words to subjects in a dichotic listening experiment.
       The pairs of words were presented at either a slow or a fast rate and subjects were given a probe
       recall test. The number of correct responses was plotted as a function of the serial position of the
       probe and also as a function of recall delay. The results showed
       a.   an interaction between presentation rate and serial position
       b.   no interaction between presentation rate and recall delay
       c.   an interaction between presentation rate and recall delay
       d.   both a and b

ANSWER: *D*

22.   Hypothetical results from a dichotic listening experiment are presented in the figure below.

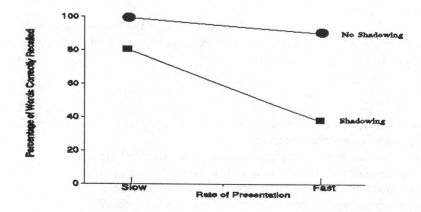

This pattern of results shows there is an interaction. This interaction

    a.   can be interpreted meaningfully
    b.   cannot be interpreted because there is a ceiling effect
    c.   cannot be interpreted because there is a floor effect
    d.   both b and c

ANSWER: *B*

23.   Broadbent and Gregory (1963) used a dichotic listening task, in which _____ were presented
to one ear and _____ was presented to the other ear.
    a.   digits; white noise
    b.   digits; words
    c.   digits; signal-detection task
    d.   tones; white noise

ANSWER: *C*

24.   Hypothetical results from a dichotic listening experiment are presented in the figure.

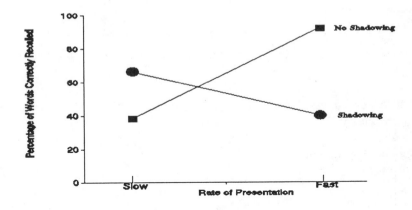

This pattern of results shows there is an interaction. This interaction
    a.   can be interpreted meaningfully
    b.   cannot be interpreted because there is a ceiling effect
    c.   cannot be interpreted because there is a floor effect
    d.   both b and c

ANSWER: *A*

25.   There is a(n) _____ relation between speed and accuracy
        a.   direct
        b.   indirect
        c.   inverse
        d.   complex

ANSWER: *C*

26.   Speed-accuracy tradeoffs pose a particular problem whenever
        a.   error rates are not systematically related to the independent variable
        b.   error rates are systematically related to the independent variable but there is no effect of the
              independent variable on reaction time
        c.   error rates increase as reaction time increases
        d.   error rates increase as reaction time decreases

ANSWER: *D*

27.   Theios (1972) was concerned with the effect of the probability that a stimulus might occur upon
        reaction time to the stimulus. On the basis of the results of his experiment, Theios concluded that
        stimulus probability had no effect upon reaction time. However, this conclusion was not warranted
        because of the problem of
        a.   scale attenuation
        b.   speed-accuracy trade-off
        c.   confounding
        d.   an inappropriate scale of measurement

ANSWER: *B*

28.   When plotting the dependent variable as a function of the independent variable, the strongest form
        of interaction is reflected in
        a.   parallel lines
        b.   nonparallel lines that do not intersect
        c.   lines that intersect
        d.   curved lines

ANSWER: *C*

29.   Attentional demand can be increased by
        a.   varying the number of alternatives in a choice reaction task
        b.   varying the presentation rate of a series of stimuli
        c.   increasing task complexity
        d.   all of the above

ANSWER: *D*

30. When a confound exists in an experiment, it places restrictions on
    a. statements made about causation
    b. interpretations of the main effects
    c. interpretations of the interactions
    d. all of the above

ANSWER: *D*

31. In contrast to Donders' subtractive method, Sternberg's additive factors method does not
    a. make statements about causation
    b. estimate the time required by a processing stage
    c. indicate how the processing stages are related
    d. use reaction time as a dependent measure

ANSWER: *B*

32. In a reaction-time task, the _____ function of the stimulus tells which response should be executed and the _____ function tells when the response should be executed.
    a. imperative; informative
    b. informative; imperative
    c. imperative; psychological
    d. psychological; imperative

ANSWER: *B*

True-False

33. Confounding occurs when an uncontrolled factor covaries or changes together with an independent variable.

ANSWER: *T*

34. When more than one independent variable can account for obtained results, we say that the variables interact.

ANSWER: *F*

35. An interaction occurs when more than one independent variable is manipulated in an experiment and the results depend upon the combination of these variables.

ANSWER: *T*

36. In a Donders' C reaction task there is more than one stimulus but only one response.

ANSWER: *T*

37. Subtracting the Donders' A reaction time from the Donders' C reaction time tells us how long response selection takes.

ANSWER: *F*

38.   The main purpose of shadowing experiments is to examine the relation between psychophysics and attentional processes.

ANSWER: *F*

39.   In the Donders' B (or choice) reaction task, two stimuli are linked to one response.

ANSWER: *F*

40.   The main purpose of shadowing experiments relates to the fate (i.e., remembered or not remembered) of the message in the attended ear.

ANSWER: *T*

41.   The way the dependent variable is measured cannot create or eliminate an interaction because an interaction is either present or is not present.

ANSWER: *F*

42.   If error rates are systematically related to the independent variable then the reaction time data may be affected by a speed-accuracy trade-off.

ANSWER: *T*

43.   Broadbent and Gregory's (1963) conclusion that attention to only one task is more effective and causes better performance than paying attention to two tasks was undermined by a confound between attention and memory.

ANSWER: *T*

44.   The presence of absence of an interaction may be determined by transformations in the scale of measurement.

ANSWER: *T*

45.   An extremely unpopular dependent variable used in research on attention is reaction time.

ANSWER: *F*

46.   There is an inverse relation between the speed and accuracy of performance.

ANSWER: *T*

47.   The interstimulus interval is a dependent variable.

ANSWER: *F*

48.   Brain wave (EEG) can be used as a dependent variable in experiments examining attention.

ANSWER: *T*

Essay

49.   Describe Donders' A, B, and C reactions and their role in Donders' subtractive method.

50.   The text describes a monitoring experiment by Broadbent and Gregory (1963) that confounded memory and attentional processes. Describe the experiment, the results and explain the confounding.

51.   Define confounding. Why is confounding a serious flaw in an experiment? Give an example of an experiment that contains a confound. How could this experiment be changed to prevent such a confounding?

52.   Describe how the presence or absence of an interaction can depend on how the dependent variable is measured. Use the results from an experiment described in the text (e.g., Knight and Kantowitz, 1975).

53.   What is meant by a interaction? Give two hypothetical examples of experiments in which an interaction might be obtained. Illustrate these interactions in a figure. Finally, provide a figure illustrating an interaction that could not be eliminated by a mathematical or statistical transformation of the data.

54.   An experimental psychologist is concerned with a number of potential problems associated with the design of experiments and the interpretation of results. Briefly discuss this statement in terms of (1) the selection of independent and control variables, (2) the selection of dependent variables, (3) confounds, (4) interactions, and (5) speed-accuracy tradeoffs.

** Text Page References for Test Questions can be found in Appendix C

Conditioning and Learning

Chapter Outline

Key Terms

AB design
ABA (reversal) design
ABAB design
ABBA design
asymmetrical transfer
balanced Latin square design
between-subjects design
carry-over effect
classical conditioning
conditioned response (CR)
conditioned stimulus (CS)
contingency
counterbalancing
discriminative stimulus
fatigue effect
instrumental conditioning
large-n experiments
matched-groups design

negative contrast effect
negative reinforcing stimulus
null contingency
operant conditioning
partial reinforcement extinction effect
positive contrast effect
positive reinforcing stimulus
practice effect
punishment
random-groups design
reinforcing stimulus
simultaneous contrast
small-n experiments
split-litter technique
unconditioned response (UR)
unconditioned stimulus (US)
within-subjects design

Answers to Discussion Questions

1. *Within-subjects designs have the advantage of requiring fewer subjects than a between-subjects design. Also, because each subject serves in every experimental condition, statistical techniques can be used to estimate the portion of the total variance that is due to subjects. As a result, within-subject designs (in general) have greater statistical power than between-subjects designs. The primary disadvantage associated with a within-subjects design is that it is not possible to use a within-subjects design in cases in which performing in one condition may affect performance in another condition.   This is the problem of asymmetrical transfer or a carry-over effect. Another problem associated with within-subject designs is that subjects may detect what is expected of them in the experiment and as a result try to cooperate with the experimenter to produce the desired result. This situation is especially problematic in social psychological research. Finally, since the same subjects are tested in different conditions in the within-subject design, care must be taken to counterbalance the order of treatment conditions so as to avoid any possible confounding of factors associated with the time of testing. The two primary effects to be considered here are practice effects and fatigue effects.*

2. *The primary advantage of using a between-subjects design is that there is no problem with carry-over effects, since each subject is tested in only one condition. One disadvantage is that a between-subject design requires many more subjects than a within-subjects design. A second disadvantage is that using different subjects in each condition makes it impossible to estimate statistically what portion of the overall variance is due to subjects. This aspect of between-subjects designs makes them less sensitive to small differences in the dependent variable between treatment conditions. This problem of increased between-subject variability in the between-subjects designs is a more serious problem for research involving human subjects, since infrahuman subjects do not seem to vary in performing tasks as much as do human subjects.*

3. *(a) A between-subjects design would be best in this situation. If a within-subjects design was used there is a real possibility that there would be carry-over effects in that subjects might perform directly in the later*

group(s) as a result of participating in the early group(s). It is also likely that if a within-subjects design was used subjects could discern the goals of the experiment and as a result act differently than they would had they not figured out what the experiment was about. All of these problems would be avoided in a between-subjects design.

(b) *Within-subjects designs are preferred in reaction time (RT) studies like this one because of the greater statistical power obtained with a within-subjects design. Any differences in RT between conditions are likely to be relatively small, and differences between individuals are likely to be large in comparison. Hence it is best to use a within-subjects design so as to have greater statistical power than would be obtained using a between-subjects design. carry-over effects are not likely to be a problem so long as the range of intensities being used is not extreme.*

(c) *This experiment could be reasonably performed by using either a within-subjects or a between-subjects design, depending upon how the experiment was to be conducted. Regardless of which type of design was used the researcher would have to counterbalance across the women used as confederates in the experiment the color of the wigs used in order to avoid confounding hair color and some other feature(s) of the women (e.g., facial characteristics). If a within-subjects design were used it would also be necessary to use a fairly large number of confederates in order to minimize the likelihood that subjects would discern the goal of the experiment. If a between-subjects design were used there is less likelihood that subjects would discern the goal of the experiment. However, due to the fact that individual subject differences are likely to be large in this type of task, a very large number of subjects would be required for a between-subjects design.*

(d) *This experiment would require a between-subjects design since it is very likely that the animals would show some carry-over effects from the early training to the later training.*

4. *A balanced Latin square is a counterbalancing scheme employed with within-subjects designs. In a balanced Latin square design every condition precedes and follows every other condition an equal number of times. This type of design has the advantage of minimizing any carry-over effects since, on the average, each condition occurs at the same stage of practice.*

Balanced Latin square for three conditions

	Square 1			Square 2		
Subjects	*Order of Testing Conditions*					
	1st	2nd	3rd	1st	2nd	3rd
a	1	2	3	3	2	1
b	2	3	1	1	3	2
c	3	2	2	2	1	3

Balanced Latin square for four conditions

Subjects	*Order of Testing Conditions*			
	1st	2nd	3rd	4th
a	1	2	4	3
b	2	3	1	4
c	3	4	2	1
d	4	1	3	2

5. *Any number of variables could be listed here. Variables that could reasonably be expected to show the same effects in between- and within-subjects designs would be variables that one would not expect to*

produce any carry-over effects. Some illustrative examples are:
1. The effect of rated imagery values on the free recall of concrete nouns.
2. The effect of prior presentation/nonpresentation of a word upon subsequent visual detection thresholds for the presented/nonpresented words.
3. The effect of the type of display (analog vs. digital) on monitoring accuracy.
    Variables that might be expected to produce different results in a between-subjects is opposed to a within-subjects design are those that might produce large carry-over effects or that might allow the subjects to discern the aim of the experiment. Illustrative examples include:
1. The type of verbal reinforcement used in a study on verbal conditioning.
2. The amount of deprivation in an experiment on drive levels.
3. The discriminability of tones is a psychoacoustic signal detection experiment.

6. *The AB design is a basic design where A represents the baseline condition before an experimental treatment and B represents the condition after the independent variable is administered. The AB design is very susceptible to a variety of confoundings. The primary reason is that the experimental treatment during the B phase may be confounded by any number of other factors. Some of these factors may be apparent, others may not. Consequently, changes during the B phase may be cause by the experimental treatment, or other confounded factors. A basic factor confounded with the treatment condition is the passage of time. That is, a similar change may occur if nothing is done during the B phase, as in a control condition. Many kinds of confoundings may arise with the use of a AB design. For example, benefits of therapy during the B phase may be cause directly by the therapist's work or by other factors such as social interactions that arise during the patient's trip to the therapist.*

Lecture Suggestion

A major area in which the principles of classical conditioning have been applied to human learning is behavior therapy. Three types of behavior therapy that apply the principles of classical conditioning to the treatment of behavioral problems are systematic desensitization (Wolpe, 1958, 1961), implosive therapy or "flooding" (Stampfl and Levis, 1967), and aversive therapy.

The goal of systematic desensitization is to try to remove the anxiety or fear response that is connected with a certain class of situations (e.g., great heights) by a gradual process of counterconditioning. In counterconditioning the patient learns to associate a response with the fear provoking situation that is incompatible with the fear response. The response that is usually used is deep muscle relaxation. In classical
conditioning terminology, the anxiety-provoking situation is considered the CS and the fear or anxiety is the CR that is elicited by the situation. Through counterconditioning the patient learns to associate a new CR (muscular relaxation) to the CS. (See Kazdin and Wilcoxin, 1976, for a review of the
systematic desensitization literature.)

In implosive therapy, or "flooding", the principle of extinction is used to rid patients of their fear reactions. Here again, the fear-eliciting situation is considered a CS and the fear or anxiety is considered the CR. In implosive therapy the patient is asked to imagine himself in the most fear-evoking situation and to experience all of the emotion associated with that situation. The basic idea behind implosive therapy is to extinguish the association between the CS and CR.

In aversive therapy a patient is presented with an aversive stimulus (e.g., a painful but noninjurious electric shock) while he is engaging in the unwanted behavior (e.g., while an alcoholic is drinking an alcoholic beverage). In this situation, the aversive stimulus is the US, the unwanted behavior is the CS, the pain is the UR, and the fear elicited by the US is the CR. The idea behind aversive therapy is that after pairing the aversive stimulus (US) with the unwanted behavior (CS), the CS alone will come to elicit the aversive CR (fear or anxiety). (See Vogler et al., 1977, for an example of aversive therapy.)

Finally, note that these forms of therapy are not accepted as useful by all clinicians, and that they are presented only as illustrative examples of how the principles of classical conditioning can be applied to modify human behavior.

References

Kazdin, A.E. & Wilcoxin, L.A. (1976). Systematic desensitization and nonspecific treatment effects: A methodological evaluation. Psychological Bulletin, 83, 729-758.

Stampfl, T. G. & Levise, D.J. (1976). Essentials of implosive therapy: A learning-theory-based psychodynamic behavior therapy. Journal of Abnormal Psychology, 72, 496-503.

Vogler, R.E., Weissbach, T.A., Compton, J. V., & Martin, G.T. (1977). Integrated techniques for problem drinkers in the community. Journal of Consulting and Clinical Psychology, 45, 267-279.

Wolpe, J. (1958). Psychotherapy by Reciprocal Inhibition. Stanford, CA: Stanford University Press.

Wolpe, J. (1961). The systematic desensitization treatment of neuroses. Journal of Nervous and Mental Diseases, 132, 89-203.

Demonstration

If instrumental conditioning apparatus is available a good demonstration would be to use the method of successive approximations to train a rat to press a response lever or a pigeon to peck at the response key. In both cases the animal should be magazine trained prior to the demonstration.

Alternatively, if an animal is available that has already been trained to respond (i.e., to bar-press or key-peck) then a good demonstration would be to show how a discriminative stimulus can bring the subjects responding under stimulus control. For this discrimination training use the stimulus lights in the training apparatus and reinforce the subject for responding when the stimulus light is on, and do not reinforce responding when the stimulus light is not on.

Experimental Dilemmas

1. An experimental psychologist wanted to test the effects of three levels of aversive noise on rats' alley running speed. The subjects were placed at one end of a straight alley, and when the start box was opened the rat could run to the other end of the alley where there was a goal box. When the start box was opened the aversive noise was turned on, and the noise was turned off when the subject entered the goal box.

    The noise levels being used were not intense enough to cause permanent damage to the subjects, so the psychologist decided to use a within-subjects design. Counterbalancing was achieved through the use of a balanced Latin square, as indicated below.

<table>
<tr><td></td><td colspan="3">**Order of Testing**</td></tr>
<tr><td>Group</td><td>1st</td><td>2nd</td><td>3rd</td></tr>
<tr><td>a</td><td>1</td><td>2</td><td>3</td></tr>
<tr><td>b</td><td>2</td><td>3</td><td>1</td></tr>
<tr><td>c</td><td>3</td><td>1</td><td>2</td></tr>
</table>

Three subjects were assigned randomly to each of the three groups. For each order of testing the subjects were given five trials, and the average time to run the alley for those five trials served as the subjects' score for that condition.

The results of the experiment showed several interesting differences among the three groups. When the researcher wrote up the results of this experiment he argued that the design he employed was a valid design that ruled out alternative explanations. Do you agree with this argument? What features of this design make it a good experiment? Are there any flaws in the design?

ANSWER: *The one major flaw with this design is that when there are an odd number of treatment conditions to be used in a within-subjects design, the counterbalancing requires two balanced Latin squares. With a single balanced Latin square every condition does not precede and follow every other condition equally often (i.e., treatment condition 3 follows condition 2 twice, and it never follows condition 1.)*

2. A pharmaceutical company had developed a new drug that it claimed would improve a person's learning ability. The drug was administered in pill form, and the company claimed that the effect of the drug would last for 48 hours. In order to demonstrate the effectiveness of the drug, the company wanted to test the drug using human subjects, but since the drug was still an experiment product the company could only test a small number of people. To make the experiment as sensitive as possible the drug researchers used a within-subjects design. Since the effects of the drug are so long-lasting it was decided to use a testing scheme in which first the subject was tested without the drug, then the drug was administered, and then the person was retested. Since the drug was only administered after the first test and before the second test, the researchers felt confident that any difference in performance levels between the two tests would accurately reflect the effect of the drug on performance.

Ten adult males served as subjects in experiment. In the first (nondrug) phase, 5 of the subjects were presented with a puff of air to the eye (UCS) that was preceded by a tone (CS). (The UCR was an eye-blink.) Interspersed within these conditioning trails were test trails in which the tone alone was presented. The dependent variable was how many conditioning trials it took until the subject made the CR (eyeblink) on 5 consecutive test trials. After the subject reached this criterion he was given 50 extinction trials in which the tone alone was presented. These extinction trials were included so as to prevent any conditioning in the first phase of the experiment from affecting performance in the second (drugged) phase.

Following this, the subjects were given the drug, and then waited two hours for the drug to take effect. In the last phase of the experiment the subjects participated in a second eyeblink conditioning experiment. This time the CS was a buzzer, and again the dependent variable was the number of trials to criterion.

Finally, in order to counterbalance the order of the CS across the first and second conditioning phases, 5 additional subjects were given the buzzer as the CS in phase one and the tone as a CS in phase two.

Results showed that there was a reliable effect of drugged versus nondrugged, with the drugged condition taking fewer trials to reach criterion. Also, there was no reliable effect of order of tone versus buzzer, with both groups of 5 subjects showing the same speed of learning in both phases.

The researchers concluded that these data indicate that their drug does speed up learning. Do you agree or disagree with this conclusion? Why or why not?

ANSWER: *Disagree. There are very likely to be carry-over effects in an eyeblink conditioning experiment. Hence the difference between phase one and phase two could have been due to these carry-over effects. For example, following the extinction after phase one there was a long delay. There could have easily been spontaneous recovery effects following this long delay, and that could affect phase two performance.*

Questions

Multiple Choice

1. In instrumental conditioning, behavior is instrumental in producing the
    a. reward.
    b. US.
    c. unconditioned response.
    d. conditioned response.

ANSWER: *A*

2. Ivan Pavlov is best known for discovering
    a. operant conditioning
    b. instrumental conditioning
    c. classical conditioning
    d. both a and b

ANSWER: *C*

3. For classical conditioning to occur, it is important for the CS ____ the US.
    a. to coincide with
    b. to predict
    c. to be similar to
    d. to be presented after

ANSWER: *B*

Questions 4-8 are based upon the following scenario. When Kent got his puppy (Bill) he began feeding him dry dog food. Kent noticed that every time he put food in the dog's dish, Bill would salivate. When Bill got older, Kent switched to canned dog food. In a few days Kent noticed that whenever he used his electric can opener, Bill would salivate.

4. A psychologist would call the food that was poured into Bill's food dish the
    a. unconditioned stimulus
    b. conditioned stimulus
    c. positive reinforcer
    d. primary reinforcer

ANSWER: *A*

5. A psychologist would call Bill's salivating when food was poured into his dish the
    a. unconditioned response
    b. unconditioned stimulus
    c. conditioned stimulus
    d. shaped response

ANSWER: *A*

6.   When Bill was being fed the dry dog food, the sound of the electric can opener being operated was a(n)
        a.   conditioned stimulus
        b.   unconditioned stimulus
        c.   discriminative stimulus
        d.   neutral stimulus

ANSWER: *D*

7.   When Bill started to salivate when he heard the electric can opener being operated, that salivating is called a(n)
        a.   unconditioned response
        b.   conditioned response
        c.   Pavlovian response
        d.   latent anticipatory response

ANSWER: *B*

8.   After Bill had started to salivate when he heard the electric can opener being operated, the sound of the can opener being operated would be called a(n)
        a.   unconditioned stimulus
        b.   conditioned stimulus
        c.   neutral stimulus
        d.   discriminative stimulus

ANSWER: *B*

9.   When one event predicts another, a _____ is said to exist between the two events.
        a.   conditioned response
        b.   unconditioned response
        c.   contingency
        d.   reward

ANSWER: *C*

10.   "If an operant response is made and followed by a reinforcing stimulus, the probability that the response will occur again is increased." This statement defines the
        a.   Law of Parsimony
        b.   Law of Effect
        c.   Thorndike's Law
        d.   Pavlov's reinforcement principle

ANSWER: *B*

11.   Reinforcing an organisms behavior that is closer and closer to the desired behavior is called
        a.   response discrimination
        b.   contingent reinforcement
        c.   shaping
        d.   method of generalization

ANSWER: *C*

12.   A stimulus that informs the organism when a behavior will be reinforced is called the
        a.   discriminative stimulus
        b.   environmental response cue
        c.   conditioned stimulus
        d.   secondary reinforcer

ANSWER: *A*

13.   Skinner called Pavlovian conditioning
        a.   classical conditioning.
        b.   instrumental conditioning.
        c.   operant conditioning.
        d.   respondent conditioning.

ANSWER: *D*

14.   An important dependent variable commonly used in classical conditioning is
        a.   frequency of responding
        b.   amplitude of the response
        c.   speed of responding
        d.   response latency

ANSWER: *D*

15.   Which of the following independent variables may be used in either classical or instrumental
        conditioning?
        a.   reinforcement schedules
        b.   delay of time between response and reinforcement
        c.   magnitude of the reinforcement
        d.   all of the above

ANSWER: *D*

16.   Which of the following is not a basic measure of animal learning but is rather a derived measure
        of learning?
        a.   pseudoconditioning
        b.   resistance of extinction
        c.   frequency of responding
        d.   magnitude of the response

ANSWER: *A*

17.   The appropriate control for pseudoconditioning is to employ a conditioning group and a control group. The animals in the control group are exposed to the same number of CS and US presentations as the animals in the experimental group, but in the control group.
       a.   the CS never precedes the US
       b.   the CS is different than the CS in the conditioning group
       c.   the CS and US presentations are unpaired and presented randomly
       d.   the US is different than the US in the conditioning group

ANSWER: *C*

18.   An organism is said to be under stimulus control when it responds correctly and consistently in the _____ of a discriminative stimulus.
       a.   presence
       b.   absence
       c.   presence and absence
       d.   none of the above

ANSWER: *A*

19.   A researcher wants to conduct an animal learning experiment using 40 subjects in a between-subjects design. The researcher decides to randomly assign the subjects to the four different conditions so that
       a.   subjects from the same litter will not be tested together
       b.   the data will be easier to analyze than if subjects were assigned on any other basis
       c.   the results will be more generalizable
       d.   the groups will be equivalent prior to the manipulation of the independent variable

ANSWER: *D*

20.   If there is in fact a small, but real, difference between treatment conditions, which design is the most likely to detect that difference?
       a.   within-subjects design
       b.   random-groups design
       c.   between-groups design
       d.   split-litter design

ANSWER: *A*

21.   A matched-groups design differs from a between-subjects design in that in the matched-group design
       a.   some performance measure is used to match subjects across conditions
       b.   subjects are matched across groups on their scores on the dependent variable
       c.   the experimenter attempts to reduce the variability among observations between groups
       d.   both a and c

ANSWER: *D*

22. Which of the following is (are) the disadvantage(s) of using a within-subjects design?
    a. the variability due to subjects cannot be estimated statistically
    b. treatment order effects
    c. a large number of subjects is required
    d. both a and c

ANSWER: *B*

23. Which of the following is (are) the advantage(s) of using a between-subjects design?
    a. the variability due to subjects can be estimated statistically
    b. there can be no treatment order effects
    c. only a small number of subjects are required
    d. both a and d

ANSWER: *B*

24. For which of the following situations would a within-subjects design be the most appropriate design?
    a. we want to know whether training rats to learn one maze will aid learning a second different maze
    b. we want to know whether rats prefer a solution sweetened with sugar more than a solution sweetened with saccharin
    c. we want to know whether a particular brain lesion will affect a rats preference for a sweet solution
    d. we want to know whether ingesting alcohol will increase rats preference for an alcoholic drink over a non-alcoholic drink

ANSWER: *B*

25. The primary reason why within-subjects designs are preferred over between-subjects designs is that
    a. fewer subjects are required
    b. there are no treatment order effects
    c. error variability is reduced
    d. the subjects are less likely to figure out the purpose of the experiment

ANSWER: *C*

26. The split-litter technique can be used in animal learning research for which experimental design?
    a. matched-groups design
    b. between-subjects design
    c. within-subjects design
    d. random-groups design

ANSWER: *A*

27.   If you wanted to train your puppy to perform a new trick on command, which of the following suggestions should you employ?
        a.   you should only train your dog after he has been fed
        b.   you should reinforce your dog for successive approximations to the behavior you want him to perform
        c.   you should teach your dog a discriminative stimulus
        d.   both b and c

ANSWER: *D*

28.   Counterbalancing is a technique used to vary the order of conditions in an experiment in order to prevent which of the following from being confounded with treatment conditions
        a.   fatigue effects
        b.   treatment order effects
        c.   practice effects
        d.   all of the above

ANSWER: *D*

29.   In order to avoid a large practice effect that may occur early in training, the experimenter should
        a.   use an ABBA design so that each condition would be tested (on the average) at the same time
        b.   use more than one counterbalancing scheme, such as giving half of the subjects ABBA and the other half BAAB
        c.   give subjects practice trials before beginning the experiment proper in order to stabilize performance before the experimental conditions of interest are introduced
        d.   both b and c

ANSWER: *D*

30.   The negative contrast effect obtained in Bower's experiment on simultaneous contrast refers to the finding that rats who receive both large and small rewards ran
        a.   just as fast for the small rewards as rats who received only the small rewards
        b.   faster for the small rewards than did rats who received only the small rewards
        c.   slower for the small rewards than did rats who only received the small rewards
        d.   faster for the large rewards than did the rats who only received the large rewards

ANSWER: *C*

31.   Pseudoconditioning refers to
        a.   a long-term elevation in the amplitude of the conditioned response that is due to an association between the CS and US
        b.   a temporary elevation in the amplitude of the conditioned response that is due to an association between the CS and US
        c.   a temporary elevation in the amplitude of the conditioned response that is not due to an association between the CS and US
        d.   none of the above

ANSWER: *C*

32. A partial reinforcement schedule produces learning that
    a. extinguishes more rapidly than learning on a continuous reinforcement schedules
    b. extinguishes at the same rate as does learning on a continuous reinforcement schedule
    c. does not extinguish as rapidly as does learning on a continuous reinforcement schedule
    d. can not be compared to the learning produced on a continuous reinforcement schedule

ANSWER: *C*

33. In an eye-conditioning experiment, the _____ is the air puff, the _____ is the blinking, and the _____ is the light that precedes the air puff.
    a. CS; UCR; UCS
    b. UCS; UCR; CS
    c. UCR; CS; UCS
    d. CS; UCS; UCR

ANSWER: *B*

34. A _____ is one in which the reinforcer is independent of behavior.
    a. positive contingency
    b. negative contingency
    c. null contingency
    d. conditioned independency

ANSWER: *C*

True-False

35. A discriminative stimulus is a stimulus that the animal finds reinforcing and is used to shape the animal's behavior.

ANSWER: *F*

36. In operant conditioning the response comes before or after the reinforcer.

ANSWER: *F*

37. An important dependent variable commonly used in Pavlovian conditioning is the amplitude of the response.

ANSWER: *T*

38. Dependent variables commonly used in animal learning research include frequency of responding, latency of responding and amplitude of the response.

ANSWER: *T*

39.   Resistance to extinction is a basic measure of the effectiveness of some independent variable on learning.

ANSWER: *T*

40.   Fatigue and practice effects are more serious for within-subjects designs than between-subjects designs.

ANSWER: *F*

41.   Pseudoconditioning refers to an elevation in the amplitude of the conditioned response that is due to the association between the CS and US.

ANSWER: *F*

42.   A between-subjects design with human subjects can be less sensitive than a between-subjects design with animals because it is easier to match animal subjects on relevant variables than it is to match human subjects.

ANSWER: *T*

43.   Within-subjects designs are usually more sensitive than between-subjects designs in detecting small differences between conditions on the dependent variable.

ANSWER: *T*

44.   Disadvantages of using a between-subjects design are treatment order effect cannot be controlled and more subjects are usually required.

ANSWER: *F*

45.   In animal research, the split-litter technique is used for random-groups designs.

ANSWER: *F*

46.   The partial reinforcement extinction effect refers to the phenomenon that partial reinforcement schedules produce learning that extinguishes more rapidly than does learning on continuous reinforcement schedules.

ANSWER: *F*

47.   A balanced Latin square design ensures that each testing condition is followed and preceded equally often by every other condition.

ANSWER: *T*

48.   The earliest examples of classical conditioning were experiments by Thorndike.

ANSWER: *F*

49.   The balanced Latin square design is the only counterbalancing scheme in which each condition precedes and follows every other condition equally often.

ANSWER: *T*

50.   Classical and instrumental conditioning are usually seen as obeying the same principles.

ANSWER: *F*

51.   In respondent conditioning, the experimenter waits until the animal makes the desired response and then rewards it.

ANSWER: *F*

Essay

52.   How does the intensity of the conditioned stimulus affect acquisition of a conditioned response? Outline experimental findings that support your answer.

53.   What are the primary advantages and disadvantages of within- subjects and between-subjects designs? What techniques are used to try to help solve some of the problems associated with within-subjects designs?

54.   Why is Skinner's use of the terms operant conditioning and respondent conditioning appropriate? Explain the difference between conditioning procedures.

55.   How does a matched-subjects design try to incorporate some of the advantages of the within-subjects design into a between-subjects design?

56.   Describe how principles of conditioning can explain the development of behavioral problems in children and how these same principles can be applied to the treatment of the problems.

57.   Grice and Hunter (1964) completed an experiment designed to resolve the issue of whether the intensity of the conditioned stimulus affects acquisition of the conditioned response. Briefly describe the (1) rationale, (2) design, (3) procedure, (4) results, and (5) conclusions of their experiment.

** Text Page References for Test Questions can be found in Appendix C

Remembering and Forgetting

Chapter Outline

Key Terms

amnesia
Brown-Patterson technique
ceiling effect
cross-over interaction
explicit memory
floor effect
forced-choice recognition test
free recall
generality of results
higher-order interaction
implicit memory
interaction
levels of processing
main effect
mixed design

nonsense syllable
paired-associate recall
priming
recall
recognition
savings method
scale-attenuation effects
serial recall
subject representativeness
tetrahedral model of memory experiments
transfer appropriate processing
trials to criterion
variable representativeness
word fragment completion task
yes/no recognition test

Answers to Discussion Questions

1.   *Situation 1. Some psychologists interested in the study of memory often conduct research with amnesic patients. For any of a number of reasons amnesics have great difficulty in learning new information. That is, they experience very rapid forgetting. It is quite common for these patients to be unable to recall any items from a previously presented list of words on a recall test. Such rapid forgetting almost always produces floor effects in recall performance. One way to overcome this problem is to test the amnesics in some way other than measuring percent correct on a recall test. A word fragment completion task might be used in which subjects are asked to fill in letters in order to form a word from a fragment (e.g., assassin from __ s s __ s s i __). Researchers using this task often find that amnesics are better able to complete previously presented words than words not presented by the experimenter, even though they might not be able to report the words on a recall test.*

Situation 2. Researchers studying recognition memory often have the problem of finding ceiling effects in performance on recognition tests. That is, subjects sometimes score almost perfectly on forced choice tests in which they must choose a target from several alternatives. One way in which this problem may be addressed is to make the choice more difficult by using distractor items that are more similar to the correct answer. For instance, if a subjects saw the word "sofa" in a list of words in a memory experiment and then had to select it out of a group of words on a test, it would be more difficult to select "sofa" from the alternatives "couch", "sofa", "divan", and "loveseat" which are semantically similar to one another than it would from the alternatives "dog", "sofa", "beach", and "orange" which bear no apparent similarity to one another.

2.   *When a result fails to generalize to a new setting, scientists usually conduct further research to find out why this is so. Quite often the subsequent investigation of the issue leads to a broader understanding of the world than was originally expected, even though the science itself might undergo a period of crisis until the issue is resolved. A famous example of this was the Copernican revolution in astronomy. Prior to Copernicus' theory, the Ptolemaic system of compounded circles was used and in most cases it worked quite well in making predictions of star and planet positions. However, problems arose when it was found that Ptolemy's predictions did not conform with the best available observations in some circumstances such as the precision of the equinoxes. Extensive modifications were made to Ptolemy's theory in order to account for these problems. These modifications eventually led to Copernicus' theory which was able*

to make more accurate predictions under a wide variety of circumstances even though it was a much simpler theory than its predecessor.

3. *Multifactor experiments allow the researcher to examine simultaneously the effects of several variables on one another. It is possible to gather information in one multifactor experiment that might otherwise have required several single factor experiments. In addition, the use of multifactor designs allows the experimenter to determine whether the effects of one variable generalize to other situations created by the inclusion of extra experimental variables.*

Lecture Suggestion

Although amnesic patients are seldom able to recognize information as being familiar by relying on their memories for past episodes, it is not uncommon for them to be able to use that same information in order to perform some perceptual or motor task. For instance, the prior presentation of an intact picture has been shown to enhance identification of an impoverished version of that same picture even though the amnesics tested denied having any past experience with the picture (Milner, Corkin, & Teuber, 1968). Several researchers have suggested that this dissociation between memory and awareness may be shown to generalize to populations of normal subjects. (See Jacoby & Witherspoon, 1982, for a review). An example of this generalization was illustrated in a paper published by Tulving, Schacter, and Stark (1982). Subjects were presented with a list of words and were later given a recognition test and a word fragment completion task. Subjects were better able to complete the word fragments for those items that had been presented for study than for words not seen in the experiment. Word fragment completion performance was shown to be independent of recognition performance, indicating a dissociation between memory and awareness such as that observed with amnesics. Furthermore, evidence of the separation of recognition and word fragment completion performance was reflected in the fact that recognition performance declined dramatically over the course of a one week delay whereas word fragment completion performance remained unchanged.

References

Jacoby, L. L. & Witherspoon, D. (1982). Remembering without awareness. Canadian Journal of Psychology, 36, 300-324.
Milner, B., Corkin, S., & Teuber, H. L. (1968). Further analysis of the hippocampal amnesia syndrome. Neuropsychologia, 6, 215-234.
Tulving, E., Schacter, D.L., & Stark, H.A. (1982). Priming effects in word fragment completion are independent of recognition memory. Journal of Experimental Psychology: Learning, Memory, & Cognition, 4, 336-342.

Demonstration

It is often found that people are able to remember large amounts of information if they can find some meaningful way to "chunk" the information into smaller units. Say the following series of numbers aloud to the class and have them recall the list in order afterwards.

1492177619411812

Students will no doubt experience difficulty in correctly recalling the entire series of digits. However, point out that this list of 16 numbers may also be encoded as four important historical dates: 1492; 1776; 1941; and 1812 which are easily remembered. Students will find that many otherwise burdensome quantities of information may be remembered when chunked into more manageable units, although the chunking process may require a little imagination in some cases.

Experimental Dilemmas

1. An investigator wanted to determine whether the level at which a word is processed would affect its probability of being recalled. Specifically, it was thought that words would be better recalled if they were processed to a deep level than if they were processed only shallowly. The experimenter tested three groups of subjects. Subjects in each group performed a different task on the words as they were presented. Subjects in the graphemic group decided whether each word contained a particular letter. The phonemic group's task was to determine whether the presented word rhymed with another word that they were given. The semantic group decided whether the presented word had a meaning similar to another word. The semantic task was believed to require a deeper level of processing than the phonemic task which was thought to involve deeper processing than the graphemic task. Each subject saw the same list of five words and each word was presented for 15 seconds. Following presentation of the list, subjects were asked to recall the words in any order they wished. The following results were obtained.

Type of Task	% Recall
Semantic	90%
Phonemic	98%
Graphemic	99%

The experimenter concluded that the level of processing of the presented words produced no effect on recall performance since the level of recall did not differ among the three groups. Do you agree with this conclusion? If not, why?

ANSWER: *This conclusion that the level of processing produced no effect on recall performance is precarious since there appears to be a ceiling effect in the present experiment. That is, performance in all three conditions is virtually perfect. This problem might be overcome by presenting longer input lists or by presenting each individual word for a shorter period of time. If recall scores were thus brought down within the range of the dependent measure you might very well find differences in performance as a function of the type of orienting task performed on the items at input.*

2. A researcher hypothesizes that subjects will be able to recall words better when given instructions to form images of the words during presentation than if given no special instructions. In addition the experimenter wishes to examine the effects of delaying the recall test for different periods of time. It is expected that recall performance will drop with increased delay but it is not known how this variable might interact with the encoding manipulation. Two groups of subjects are tested: The Imagery group is instructed to form mental images of each word as it is presented, but the No Imagery group is given no explicit instructions. All subjects are presented with the same list of 50 concrete nouns at the rate of 10 seconds each. Each of the two groups is divided so that half of the subjects are given a free

recall test one hour after presentation and half are given a free recall test one week later. All subjects are allowed 20 minutes for the recall test. The results obtained are presented below.

		Instructions	
		Imagery	No Imagery
	1 Hour	75%	50%
Delay	1 Week	50%	25%

There was a main effect of instruction condition and of delay condition but there was no instruction x delay interaction. From these data the experimenter concluded that memory performance is enhanced when subjects are instructed to form mental images of input items and that performance decreases as the delay between input and test increases, but that the delay manipulation does not differentially affect performance as a function of input condition. Do you agree with these conclusions? If not, why?

ANSWER: *Agree.*

Questions

Multiple Choice

1. On an implicit word fragment completion test, 47 percent of the fragments in the studied condition were completed and 23 percent of fragments in the nonstudied condition were completed. The amount of priming is _____ percent.
   a. 24
   b. 70
   c. 23
   d. 47

ANSWER: *A*

2. Why did Ebbinghaus consider it important to use nonsense syllables in his memory experiments?
   a. He did not think that CVCs would be difficult to learn.
   b. He wanted to reduce the likelihood that linguistic associations could be formed among the stimuli.
   c. He wanted to minimize savings in learning stimulus lists for the second time.
   d. He was studying retroactive interference.

ANSWER: *B*

3. The conscious recollection of events in one's life relies on _____ memory.
   a. explicit
   b. implicit
   c. episodic
   d. both a and c

ANSWER: *D*

4.   The use of nonsense syllables was not a perfect solution to the problems Ebbinghaus hoped to avoid
        by their use because
        a.   some of his nonsense syllables were words
        b.   meaning may be attached to nonsense syllables
        c.   some of his nonsense syllables sounded like words
        d.   all of the above

ANSWER: *D*

5.   Remembering information over a duration of several seconds involves _____ memory.
        a.   implicit
        b.   short-term
        c.   intermediate
        d.   long-term

ANSWER: *B*

6.   Ebbinghaus found that even when he could not recall any of the stimuli in a previously studied list,
        he often
        a.   relearned the list faster than the original learning
        b.   showed savings
        c.   had more trials to criterion
        d.   both a and b

ANSWER: *D*

7.   Ebbinghaus measured forgetting as a function of retention interval and found that
        a.   forgetting is very slow at first but then speeds up.
        b.   forgetting is rapid at first and the levels off.
        c.   the amount of forgetting decreases steadily with retention interval.
        d.   the amount of forgetting remains constant across all retention intervals.

ANSWER: *B*

8.   A memory test in which subjects recall items in any order they choose is called a
        a.   yes/no recall test.
        b.   paired associate recall test.
        c.   free recall test.
        d.   serial recall test.

ANSWER: *C*

9.   Answering questions about the movie you saw last night would involve _____ memory.
        a.   long-term
        b.   implicit
        c.   explicit
        d.   both a and c

ANSWER: *D*

10. Multiple choice tests are similar to _____tests and essay tests are similar to _____tests.
    a. yes/no recognition; free recall
    b. forced choice recognition; serial recall
    c. forced choice recognition; free recall
    d. yes/no recognition; serial recall

ANSWER: *C*

11. Which of the following is not true?
    a. There is a clearcut distinction between recall and recognition.
    b. Forced choice tests are preferred to yes/no tests because correcting for guessing is less of a problem with the forced choice procedure.
    c. The number of errors made on a memory test is frequently used as a dependent variable in memory experiments.
    d. a and c

ANSWER: *B*

12. _____ memory refers to the expression of past learning without the need for conscious effort to retrieve information from the past.
    a. Explicit
    b. Implicit
    c. Episodic
    d. Long-term

ANSWER: *B*

13. Which of the following is an instance of proactive interference?
    a. You learned French in high school and now you confuse French words with new words that you are learning in your Latin class.
    b. You find that after taking an ASSEMBLY language computer course this semester you cannot remember commands from a FORTRAN course that you took last year.
    c. You have trouble recalling the names of your gradeschool classmates.
    d. All of the above.

ANSWER: *A*

14. Scarborough (1972) could not draw any conclusions about differential forgetting in his auditory and visual presentation conditions because
    a. performance in the auditory and visual presentation conditions was equivalent across all retention intervals.
    b. performance was virtually perfect in all conditions at the zero retention interval.
    c. performance was poorer in the auditory than in the visual presentation condition at the longer retention intervals.
    d. performance was poorer in the visual than in the auditory presentation condition at the longer retention intervals.

ANSWER: *B*

15.   In a recognition test, the dependent measure is
        a.   the number of items correctly recognized.
        b.   the number of errors.
        c.   response time.
        d.   all of the above

ANSWER: *D*

16.   Scale-attenuation effects refer to
        a.   modality effects
        b.   ceiling and floor effects
        c.   retroactive and proactive interference effects
        d.   none of the above

ANSWER: *B*

17.   Which of the following statements best summarizes the problem of scale attenuation effects.
        a.   There is no such thing as perfectly good or perfectly bad performance.
        b.   The size of the intervals of a dependent measure are unequal when you approach the extreme ends of the scale.
        c.   It is impossible to determine whether there are differences among experimental conditions when performance is polarized at either the high or low end of the scale of the dependent measure.
        d.   Most of the dependent measures used to study memory are relatively unconstrained and thus allow for easy interpretation of performance levels.

ANSWER: *C*

18.   The Brown-Peterson procedure is used to investigate _____ memory.
        a.   iconic
        b.   short-term
        c.   long-term
        d.   implicit

ANSWER: *B*

19.   One might reduce problems of ceiling and floor effects by
        a.   avoiding the use of tasks that are too easy.
        b.   avoiding the use of tasks that are too difficult.
        c.   testing pilot subjects to make sure that performance on a task will not be near the extremes of the scale.
        d.   all of the above.

ANSWER: *D*

20.   When a subject is asked to recall a list of items in order, good performance on the beginning of the list is called a _____ effect and good performance on the end of the list is a _____ effect.
   a.   proactive; retroactive
   b.   primacy; recency
   c.   proactive; recency
   d.   primacy; retroactive

ANSWER: *B*

21.   In the levels of processing framework, _____ processing involves a low level of analysis.
   a.   graphemic
   b.   phonemic
   c.   semantic
   d.   syntactic

ANSWER: *A*

22.   Which of the following is an example of a multifactor experiment?
   a.   Performance on a list-learning task is compared for male and female subjects.
   b.   Recall performance is measured for a 10 item list versus a 50 item list.
   c.   Amount of forgetting for a word list is measured as a function of number of presentations and word length.
   d.   Percent recall is compared between a group who studies a list for 20 minutes and a group who studies for only 10 minutes.

ANSWER: *C*

23.   What is an advantage of using multifactor designs?
   a.   They are exceedingly complex.
   b.   They allow us to examine the effects of several variables on one another simultaneously.
   c.   They remove concern about scale attenuation effects.
   d.   All of the above.

ANSWER: *B*

24.   Which of the following is true?
   a.   Within-subject designs eliminate differences between conditions that might otherwise be due to the fact that different people are tested in different conditions.
   b.   Experimenters should always use within-subjects designs as opposed to between-subjects designs.
   c.   Within-subjects designs eliminate counterbalancing concerns.
   d.   All of the above.

ANSWER: *A*

25.   In line with the levels of processing theory, Craik and Tulving (1975) found that recognition
       performance was best in _____ condition, worst in the _____ condition and intermediate
       in the _____ condition.
       a.   semantic; graphemic; phonemic
       b.   graphemic; phonemic; semantic
       c.   semantic; phonemic; graphemic
       d.   phonemic; graphemic; semantic

ANSWER: *A*

26.   An experiment with three different factors and three levels of each factor is called a
       _____ factorial design.
       a.   3 x 3 x 3
       b.   3 x 6
       c.   3 x 3
       d.   3 x 6 x 9

ANSWER: *A*

27.   According to Jenkin's tetrahedral model of memory experiments, researchers make choices along
       _____ dimensions.
       a.   two
       b.   four
       c.   five
       d.   eight

ANSWER: *B*

28.   Explicit measures of memory include such tests as
       a.   recognition
       b.   serial recall
       c.   priming measures
       d.   both a and b

ANSWER: *D*

29.   According to Jenkin's (1979) tetrahedral model of memory experiments, if type of test is varied in
       an experiment, the outcome can be influenced by
       a.   type of materials.
       b.   orienting tasks.
       c.   both a and b
       d.   none of the above

ANSWER: *D*

Questions 30-33 refer to this experiment: In an experiment, subjects studied a list of words and then tried to solve anagrams; for example, making the word MEMORY from the anagram EYMORM. Subjects were informed that the study and test phases were unrelated. The results indicated that more anagrams were solved when the solution word was in the prior study list than when the solution word was not in the prior study list.

30.   Performance on the anagram task provided a (an) _____measure of memory.
    a.   explicit
    b.   implicit
    c.   direct
    d.   trials-to-criterion

ANSWER: *B*

31.   The proportion of anagrams solved when the solution word was not in the prior study list
    a.   is a control condition
    b.   provides a baseline
    c.   is the nonstudied rate
    d.   all of the above

ANSWER: *D*

32.   The improvement in performance for anagrams whose solution was included in the prior study list is called
    a.   proactive interference
    b.   trials-to-criterion
    c.   priming
    d.   implicit benefit

ANSWER: *C*

33.   Each word should occur equally often as a studied word and as a nonstudied word
    a.   to avoid possible ceiling effects
    b.   to eliminate the possibility of relearning
    c.   to provide for more observations for each subject
    d.   to eliminate the possibility of item effects

ANSWER: *D*

34.   The orienting task variable described by Jenkins would include the use of
    a.   nonsense syllables.
    b.   an implicit task.
    c.   a within-subjects manipulation of a study variable.
    d.   amnesic subjects.

ANSWER: *C*

35.   Warrington and Weiskrantz found that amnesics performed _____ normals on an explicit test
        and _____ normals on an implicit test.
        a.   the same as; worse than
        b.   worse then; worse than
        c.   worse than; the same as
        d.   the same as; the same as

ANSWER: *C*

36.   In Blaxton's experiment, words were presented visually and auditorially, and free recall and word
        fragment completion tests were administered. An interaction was found between
        a.   list length and test type
        b.   modality and test type
        c.   priming and test type
        d.   percent correct and test type

ANSWER: *B*

37.   Asking subjects to count the number of vowels in a word or to form a sentence with the word is
        one way to manipulate
        a.   the type of test
        b.   the level of processing
        c.   the retrieval process
        d.   none of the above

ANSWER: *B*

38.   Two variables are said to interact when the effect of one variable _____ of the other
        variable.
        a.   is the same at the different levels
        b.   changes at the same levels
        c.   changes at different levels
        d.   is the same at the same levels

ANSWER: *C*

39.   If an independent variable has opposite effects at each level of a second independent variable, there
        is
        a.   is a main effect
        b.   not necessarily a main effect
        c.   a crossover interaction
        d.   both b and c

ANSWER: *D*

40. The method of loci and the peg-word method are
    a. mnemonic techniques
    b. mental operations for learning and retrieving information
    c. methods to improve one's memory
    d. all of the above

ANSWER: *D*

41. Even if a subject is unable to recall any words from a previously studied list, an experimenter may obtain evidence that the subject has some memory for the list by
    a. measuring the trials to criterion to relearn the list and comparing it with the number of trials needed to learn the list the first time
    b. measuring the savings in relearning the list a second time
    c. presenting the subject with the first three letters of each word at the time of recall
    d. all of the above

ANSWER: *D*

42. The theory that performance on a test will benefit to the extent that knowledge acquired during study must match knowledge required by the test is known as
    a. levels of processing.
    b. Jenkins' tetrahedral model.
    c. transfer appropriate processing.
    d. none of the above

ANSWER: *C*

True-False

43. Ebbinghaus' savings measure revealed that information can be learned much more quickly if it has been learned on a previous occasion.

ANSWER: *T*

44. Ebbinghaus used nonsense syllables as stimuli in his memory experiments to minimize trials to criterion and maximize savings.

ANSWER: *F*

45. In a free recall test, people are required to recall information in the order it was presented but in serial recall the order of recall is irrelevant.

ANSWER: *F*

46. According to the levels of processing approach to memory, shallower levels of processing during study leads to worse memory for the experience.

ANSWER: *T*

47.   Based on Scarborough's (1972) results we can conclude that forgetting is greater for auditory than for visual presentation.

ANSWER: *F*

48.   Ebbinghaus used savings as a dependent variable in his experiments because the number of trials to criterion was constant.

ANSWER: *F*

49.   There is no way to avoid ceiling and floor effects in memory research; we just have to learn to interpret them carefully.

ANSWER: *F*

50.   In general a main effect is observed when the effect of one variable changes at different levels of a second variable.

ANSWER: *F*

51.   Variable representativeness is a problem related to the generality of the experimental conditions.

ANSWER: *T*

52.   One of the advantages of multifactor experiments is that interactions cannot be produced by scale attenuation.

ANSWER: *F*

53.   The item "TAC" is a C V C syllable.

ANSWER: *T*

54.   When interference occurs after presentation of material to be remembered it is called retroactive interference.

ANSWER: *T*

55.   In a list-learning experiment one measure of difficulty that may be used is the number of study trials needed to reach some criterion of performance.

ANSWER: *T*

56.   The term <u>memory</u> is quite narrow and refers to very specific abilities involving remembering.

ANSWER: *F*

57.   Between-subjects designs remove any differences between groups that might be due to the fact that different subjects are tested in different groups.

ANSWER: *F*

58.   The finding that pictures produce more priming than words on a word fragment completion test is known as the picture superiority effect.

ANSWER: *F*

59.   Psychologists do not need to concern themselves with the issue of generality of results as much as scientists in other disciplines.

ANSWER: *F*

60.   If there is a main effect, there must also be an interaction.

ANSWER: *F*

61.   If there is an interaction, there must also be a main effect.

ANSWER: *F*

62.   In a line graph, parallel lines indicate a main effect and an interaction.

ANSWER: *F*

63.   A line graph will not indicate whether an interaction is significant.

ANSWER: *T*

64.   Categorical variables should be plotted with line graphs.

ANSWER: *F*

65.   IQ is an interval scale.

ANSWER: *T*

66.   Weight is an interval scale.

ANSWER: *F*

67.   Blaxton found larger priming effects for words presented auditorially than for words presented visually.

ANSWER: *F*

<u>Essay</u>

68.   Describe three experimental findings that showed a dissociation between explicit and implicit memory tests.

69.   Discuss advantages and disadvantages of using multifactor designs.

70.   Describe Jenkins' (1979) tetrahedral model of memory experiments providing examples from experiments in the text.

71.   What is a modality effect? Show an example of a modality effect using a bar graph and a line graph. Briefly describe the modality effects as found by two different researchers.

72.   Describe the main ideas of Craik and Lockhart's (1972) levels of processing approach to memory. Outline an experiment that provided support for the levels of processing approach.

73.   What are mnemonic techniques. Briefly describe two different mnemonic techniques.

74.   Describe the Brown-Peterson short-term memory procedure used in Scarborough's (1972) experiment. Describe the results of this experiment.

75.   In an experiment, a group of amnesic subjects and a group of control subjects studied a list of words and an hour later were given a free recall test and an implicit word fragment completion test. The results, in percent correct, were as follows:

	Controls	Amnesics
Free Recall:	65	25
Word Fragment Completion		
Studied Words:	75	65
Nonstudied Words:	25	15

(1) Identify the independent and dependent variables.
(2) Calculate the priming scores.
(3) Graph the results in a bar and a line graph (include priming).
(4) Label all the important parts of the graphs.
(5) Are there main effects and an interaction? Is so, what kind?
(6) Briefly interpret these results.

76.   Discuss the following statement, providing specific examples: The term <u>memory</u> is broad and includes many types of memories.

77.   Distinguish between explicit and implicit memory, and short-term and long-term memory. Describe a task used by experimental psychologists to investigate each type of memory.

** Text Page References for Test Questions can be found in Appendix C

Thinking and Problem Solving

Key Terms

analogy

boundary conditions

ceiling effect

conceptual replication

direct replication

experimental control

experimental reliability

extraneous variables

feeling-of-knowing

functional fixity

incubation

insight

latency

law of effect

mapping

reliability

replicability

statistical reliability

structural consistency

subjective report

systematic replication

thought

verbal report

Answers to Discussion Questions

1. *The replication of the first experimenter's findings in another laboratory would be a more convincing argument for ESP in rats than statistical tests showing that the rats had performed above chance. Even when a finding is statistically reliable there is still some probability that it occurred by chance. This point is particularly important in light of the fact that only two rats out of 100 showed the effect. Replication is also preferable since it is important to make sure that the effects were not due to some feature of the experimental procedure such as odour cues, scoring procedures, etc. Any such idiosyncrasies, should they exist, could be eliminated in another laboratory setting.*

    The new experimenter would want to guard against the possibility of the rats using sensory cues in several ways. First, olfactory cues could be minimized by cleaning the maze after each animal has run through it. The experimenter should always open each arm of the maze on every trial even though food is only placed in one arm. This would ensure that the animals would not learn to associate the food with the sound made in placing the food in the arm. The animals should be kept in some sort of starting box before each trial such that they are unable to see which arms of the maze the food is placed in. Finally, the experimenter should be blind to the experimental hypothesis so that he or she cannot bias the outcome through differential handling of the animals, scoring procedures, etc.

2. *The evidence for negative ESP is no better than the evidence for ESP originally reported for the same reasons stated above. Again, the result should be replicated in a different laboratory.*

3. *A direct replication is an attempt to repeat an experiment under conditions identical to the original ones. A systematic replication generally encompasses all of the conditions of the original experiment but adds manipulations that might be instructive in further understanding of the phenomenon in question. A conceptual replication is a demonstration of a phenomenon under circumstances that differ greatly from those of the original experiment. All of these lie on a continuum of similarity to the original experimental conditions. The direct replication is most similar to the original and the conceptual replication is least similar to the conditions in which the phenomenon was first observed.*

4. *Although replications should be encouraged the experimenter should not be content merely to replicate someone else's finding. Once the phenomenon is shown to be replicable an experimenter should attempt additional systematic and/or conceptual replications and include those in the "package" offered for publication.*

5. *It is usually desirable to report multiple experiments on a phenomenon within a single paper so that the reader may get some idea of the size and scope of an effect as well as its boundary conditions. That is, some degree of closure is helpful wherever possible. One inherent danger in requiring multiple experiments, however, is that such a requirement may lead researchers to abandon paradigms in which experimentation is more tedious and time consuming. In order to produce more publications an experimenter may opt for more simplistic procedures and manipulations, thus avoiding certain types of potentially interesting questions. In addition, the delay involved in running extra experiments before going to publication with a result may be detrimental to the communication of new findings among researchers.*

6. *a. Verbal reports are quite useful in studying memory strategies and in fact may be the only way to ascertain what types of cues are considered to be better memory aids than others.*
    b. Chances are that very little information concerning sexual behavior will be obtained from verbal reports since people do not usually freely discuss their sex lives with strangers. Anonymous questionnaires, one type of report, may be helpful in this line of research.
    c. Although people may say that they use certain rules in making purchasing decisions, they are probably influenced by other factors that they are either unaware of or believe themselves to be immune to. This topic is better investigated experimentally by manipulating factors believed to influence buying behavior and studying their effects in controlled settings.
    d. Liking behavior may be studied using verbal reports although other converging measures should be used as well. Subjects may fail to name traits that they like in another person when in fact those traits may play an important role in liking behavior.
    e. Verbal reports are necessary to the extent that the experimenter is unable to independently verify what a subject is perceiving. However, behavioral measures are highly instructive in the study of visual illusions for the experimenter who is clever enough to create them.

Lecture Suggestion

The advent of the computer age has brought with it some interesting questions for psychologists interested in human cognition. Among these are the issue of whether we can design a machine that thinks and if we could, how we would know whether it thinks. Turing (1950) suggested that we would know that a machine thinks if it can imitate a process that would require humans to think. Turing's test for the thinking machine went as follows. A human and a computer are placed in a room and an interrogator asks questions for which the human and the computer provide answers. If the interrogator cannot distinguish between the human and the computer on the basis of their answers, then the computer is said to think. Although the imitation criterion for thinking in machines has been challenged, many would argue that computers may show us something about our own thinking processes.

Some people have tried to imitate human problem solving by writing computer programs that simulate ways in which we might attempt to solve problems ourselves. One famous example is the Logic Theorist (LT) program written by Newell, Shaw, and Simon (1958). The program was designed to discover proofs for theorems presented in <u>Principia Mathematica</u> using symbolic logic. LT was able to solve many of the first proofs in a very short time. Many of the later proofs were impossible for LT to solve, however, when the computer was not allowed to make use of earlier proofs. What does LT tell us about human problem solving? These early examples suggest that our problem solving strategies may be hierarchically arranged and may depend upon the accumulation of prior knowledge. Since LT was presented there have been similar attempts to model human cognition through computer simulation, sometimes with very favorable results.

References

Newell, A., Shaw, J. C., & Simon, H.A. (1958).   Elements of a theory of human problem solving.
    Psychological Review, 65, 151-166.
Turing, A.M. (1950). Computing machinery and intelligence. Mind, 59, 433-460.
Whitehead, A.N. & Russell, B. (1925). Principia Mathematica (2nd ed.). Cambridge: Cambridge University
    Press.

Demonstration Suggestion

In order to gain insight into how solutions to problems are obtained, read these brain teasers to the
class and have them try to provide solutions.

1. Three men staying in a hotel are told that a room costs $30. Each man gives the room clerk $10.
    After they have checked into their room, the clerk discovers that the correct price for the room is
    actually $25. The clerk gives $5 to the bellboy and tells him to return it to the guests. The bellboy
    returns $1 to each of the men and keeps $2 for himself. This means that each man has paid $9 for a
    total of $27. Since the bellboy has $2 that gives a grand total of $29. What happened to the other
    dollar for the original $30?

ANSWER: *The calculations have been confused by adding where there should have been subtracting. Each
man originally paid $10 but got back $1 so that the total left to account for is $27 rather than $30. The hotel
has $25 of that $27 and the bellboy has the other $2. You should subtract the bellboy's $2 rather than add it
to the amount of money to be accounted for.*

2. A man buys a car for $200 and sells it for $300. Later he buys it back for $400 and sells it for $500.
    How much money did he make on the whole deal?

ANSWER: *Two hundred dollars. He made $100 on each transaction. The fact that both transactions
involved the same car is irrelevant*

3. You have nine coins and know that one of them is counterfeit and weighs more than the others. How
    can you tell which is the counterfeit coin with only two weighings on a balance scale?

ANSWER: *Divide the coins into three groups of three coins each. Weigh one group of coins on each side of
the scale. If one side of the scales is lower, you know that the counterfeit coin is in that group. If the scales
balance, you know that the counterfeit coin is in the other group. Now that you know which group the
counterfeit coin is in, weigh two of the three coins from that group on the scale. If one side of the scale goes
down you know that it is the counterfeit coin. If the scales balance, you know that the third unweighed coin
is counterfeit.*

Experimental Dilemmas

1. A researcher studying developmental differences in spatial problem solving ability conducted the
    following study. Groups of either five or seven-year olds were given a ten piece jigsaw puzzle to solve
    and were told to take as long as they needed to complete the task. Subjects were shown a picture of
    what the puzzle would look like when completed. Twenty female and 20 male children were tested in
    each age group. The results showed that 90% of the seven year olds and 87% of the five year olds

were able to complete the puzzle. Since the difference in performance levels between groups was not statistically reliable, the experimenter concluded that there are no differences in spatial ability between five and seven year olds. Do you agree with this conclusion? Why or Why not?

ANSWER: *No. The experimenter may have found differences between the groups if a different dependent measure was used, such as time needed to complete the puzzle. This seems likely given that there was a small difference in performance using the original dependent variable (although it was not statistically significant).*

2.   A peanut butter company is thinking of changing the labels on its jars of peanut butter from the colorful ones used now to a more plain and less expensive design. The company is worried, however, that sales will decline if the appearance of the product is changed drastically, so they have conducted the following research studies. First, the marketing division interviewed cross-sections of potential buyers and asked them whether they would still buy the product once the new labels were used. Of those interviewed 95% said that the label change would not affect their buying habits. In addition, the company distributed jars of peanut butter with the new labels to eight test districts and found that sales were unaffected by the change. If you were in charge of deciding whether or not to switch from the fancy to the plain labels, what would your decision be?

ANSWER: *Switch. Both verbal reports and behavioral measures converge on the finding that the change in label will not affect sales.*

Questions

Multiple Choice

1.   The two approaches to the study of problem solving represent a _____ analysis and _____ analysis analogous to the ways of examining perception.
       a.   bottom-up; top-down
       b.   direct; data-driven
       c.   bottom-up; data-driven
       d.   top-down; conceptually-driven

ANSWER: *A*

2.   According to Holyoak's theory, experience with the fortress problem will help a person solve the tumor problem
       a.   in all cases.
       b.   only if the person finds correspondences between the original problem and the transfer problem.
       c.   only if the original problem immediately precedes the transfer problem.
       d.   only if the instructions are similar.

ANSWER: *B*

3.   Thorndike's puzzle boxes
        a.   were specially constructed to study problem solving in animals.
        b.   contained food as positive reinforcement.
        c.   were mazes that animals travelled through to obtain food.
        d.   were puzzles which had no solutions.

ANSWER: *A*

4.   The successful behavior exhibited by Thorndike's cats in escaping from puzzle boxes
        a.   became more systematic with repeated trials.
        b.   could initially be described as trial and error learning.
        c.   seemed accidental during the first few trials.
        d.   all of the above.

ANSWER: *D*

5.   Kohler's research on problem solving in chimpanzees
        a.   involved problems which could be solved in a simple and direct fashion.
        b.   were analogous to Thorndike's puzzle box experiments.
        c.   involved problems for which there were no immediately obvious answers.
        d.   none of the above.

ANSWER: *C*

6.   _____ means that the elements that correspond in two problems are related to each other in a way that is not inconsistent with other mappings.
        a.   Direct mapping
        b.   Indirect mapping
        c.   Structural consistency
        d.   Structural inconsistency

ANSWER: *C*

7.   Kohler's approach to problem solving in chimpanzees
        a.   emphasized the importance of insight.
        b.   emphasized the conceptual nature of problem solving.
        c.   went beyond trial and error learning.
        d.   all of the above.

ANSWER: *D*

8.   Current research and theory in thinking and problem solving
        a.   reflect the influence of earlier animal research
        b.   reflect the influence of Gestalt psychology
        c.   are concerned with replication and reliability
        d.   all of the above

ANSWER: *D*

9. An experimenter's confidence in the reliability of a result
   a. increases with the number of observations on which it is based.
   b. is highest when a between-subjects design is used.
   c. increases with the variability of the data.
   d. decreases as the power of the statistical test used to assess the result increases.

ANSWER: *A*

10. A feature common among studies of complex mental processes is that
    a. there are often very few observations per experimental condition.
    b. variability is often high.
    c. statistical power is often low.
    d. all of the above.

ANSWER: *D*

11. In Gick and Holyoak's (1980) experiments on analogical problem solving
    a. some subjects were told to use the analogous story as a hint in solving the problem.
    b. subjects rated the adequacy of proposed solutions to a problem.
    c. all subjects read a story analogous to the problem scenario before providing a solution.
    d. subjects constructed scenarios similar to those presented for study.

ANSWER: *A*

12. Holyoak's theory of structural consistency is similar to
    a. Craik and Lockhart's levels of processing approach.
    b. McClelland and Rumelhart's model of word recognition.
    c. Thorndike's trial-and-error learning.
    d. the distinction between explicit and implicit memory.

ANSWER: *B*

13. Gick and Holyoak (1980) found that the ability to solve a problem
    a. was dependent on the subject's having previously read the solution to a similar problem.
    b. was dependent on the subject being explicitly told to use the example as a hint in solving the problem.
    c. was independent of whether subjects had been told to use the story as a hint in solving the problem.
    d. Both a and b.

ANSWER: *D*

14. A result is statistically reliable if
    a. the change observed in the independent variable is not due to chance factors.
    b. the change observed in the dependent variable would only rarely occur by chance.
    c. a repetition of the experiment yields the same result.
    d. inferential statistics are used to evaluate the outcome.

ANSWER: *B*

15.   In a _____ replication, the experimenter may change the original procedure slightly by
       manipulating factors not varied in the original experiment and thus establish boundary conditions
       for the phenomenon in question.
       a.   direct
       b.   analogical
       c.   systematic
       d.   conceptual

ANSWER: *C*

16.   In the missionaries' and cannibals' problem with three missionaries and three cannibals, the
       minimum number of moves to solve the problem is
       a.   9
       b.   11
       c.   13
       d.   17

ANSWER: *B*

17.   Which of the following is true?
       a.   The failure to replicate an experimental outcome can be instructive
       b.   The issue of generality of results is independent of the problem of replicability.
       c.   Direct replications may be thought of as converging operations.
       d.   Both a and c.

ANSWER: *A*

18.   We may say that confounding has occurred when a(n) _____ variable is allowed to vary with
       the independent variable of interest.
       a.   dependent
       b.   independent
       c.   extraneous
       d.   control

ANSWER: *C*

19.   Error variance
       a.   is a problem only when there is a large number of observations per condition.
       b.   may make it difficult to detect a reliable effect of the independent variable.
       c.   is less of a problem in between-subjects designs than in within-subjects designs.
       d.   is likely to increase the power of a statistical test.

ANSWER: *B*

20. In attempting to solve a problem, the strategy of constantly moving toward the goal is call
    a. GPS
    b. means-ends analysis
    c. functional fixidity
    d. analysis of optimal solution

ANSWER: *B*

21. The fact that most people would not think of using a newspaper to clean a car windshield is an example of _____.
    a. functional fixity
    b. feeling-of-knowing
    c. systematic analogy
    d. insight

ANSWER: *A*

22. Duncker's research on the box problem showed that
    a. very few subjects were able to solve the problem in any condition.
    b. subjects were less likely to solve the problem if the boxes contained other objects than if the boxes did not contain other objects.
    c. subjects were more likely to solve the problem if the boxes contained buttons than if the boxes contained candles.
    d. the functional fixity effect was not reliable.

ANSWER: *B*

23. Adamson's research on functional fixity shows that _____ is a more sensitive dependent measure than _____.
    a. latency; verbal report
    b. percent correct; latency
    c. latency; percent correct
    d. verbal report; percent correct

ANSWER: *C*

24. Research on the feeling-of-knowing phenomenon has shown that
    a. people's judgments of their prospective ability to recognize the answer to a question are positively correlated with later recognition performance.
    b. even though people may not be able to produce the answer to a question they are fairly good at predicting whether they could recognize it if it were later presented to them.
    c. although feeling-of-knowing performance is fairly good, it is far from perfect.
    d. all of the above.

ANSWER: *D*

25.   Experimenters using verbal reports as research tools
        a.   should not use them as the sole dependent measure in an experiment.
        b.   should continue to do so since verbal reports are perfectly correlated with performance.
        c.   may find the discrepancies between verbal reports and behavioral measures to be interesting
              in and of themselves.
        d.   both a and c.

ANSWER: *D*

26.   A _____replication is more similar to the original experiment than a _____replication.
        a.   systematic; direct
        b.   direct; conceptual
        c.   conceptual; direct
        d.   conceptual; systematic

ANSWER: *B*

27.   In general, error variance _____as experimental control _____.
        a.   increases; increases
        b.   increases; decreases
        c.   decreases; increases
        d.   both a and b

ANSWER: *D*

28.   The primary independent variable in problem solving research is
        a.   the way in which the problem is presented
        b.   the percentage of subjects solving the problem
        c.   the level of the subject's IQ
        d.   the latency in solving the problem

ANSWER: *A*

29.   Even if the percentages of people solving a problem under different conditions were the same,
        differences in performance may be revealed by
        a.   the quality of the solution
        b.   the time to solve the problem
        c.   problem solving latencies
        d.   all of the above

ANSWER: *D*

30.   In problem solving research, it is often necessary to use between-subjects design in order to
        a.   avoid ceiling effects
        b.   reduce the number of subjects in the experiment
        c.   reduce the variability of observations
        d.   avoid carry-over effects

ANSWER: *D*

31.   In the Spencer and Weisberg experiment, subjects were given two training problems before solving the radiation problem. The radiation problem was administered
      a.   at the same time as the training problems
      b.   immediately after the training problems
      c.   immediately before the training problems
      d.   none of the above

ANSWER: *B*

32.   In the Spencer and Weisberg experiment, subjects were given two training problems before solving the radiation problem. They found equal amounts of transfer in the same- and different-context groups when
      a.   all three problems were administered at the same time
      b.   the radiation problem was administered immediately after the training problems
      c.   the radiation problem was administered 45 minutes after the training problems
      d.   both a and c

ANSWER: *B*

33.   In the Spencer and Weisberg experiment, subjects were given two training problems before solving the radiation problem. Subjects in the different-context condition showed no transfer when there was _____ between the training and radiation problems.
      a.   a 45 minute delay
      b.   no delay
      c.   a 35 minute delay
      d.   both a and b

ANSWER: *A*

34.   Which of the following may vary at the same time as the independent variable.
      a.   extraneous variables
      b.   control variables
      c.   nuisance variables
      d.   all of the above

ANSWER: *A*

35.   Metcalfe's results indicated that the "feeling-of-warmth" ratings that subjects gave as they attempted to solve a problem were
      a.   very accurate
      b.   very inaccurate
      c.   fluctuated drastically from the beginning to the end of the problem solving period
      d.   both b and c

ANSWER: *B*

36.   The General Problem Solver computer program by Newell and Simon
       a.   relied on a strict means-end strategy.
       b.   generated subgoals.
       c.   relied on Holyoak's theory of structural consistency.
       d.   can solve any analogical problem with enough computer time.

ANSWER: *A*

True-False

37.   Thorndike's experiments on problem solving in cats showed that the success of a correct movement
       had no effect unless food was provided as negative reinforcement.

ANSWER: *F*

38.   Thorndike observed that cats learned to escape from puzzle boxes by trial and error.

ANSWER: *T*

39.   Kohler's chimpanzees exhibited insight in problem solving.

ANSWER: *T*

40.   Current research in problem solving and thinking reflects a greater influence of behaviorism than
       of the Gestalt approach.

ANSWER: *F*

41.   Verbal reports are unacceptable as behavioral evidence.

ANSWER: *F*

42.   Between-subjects designs are frequently used in problem solving research because they allow for
       more experimental control than do within-subjects designs.

ANSWER: *F*

43.   A result is said to be reliable if a repetition of the experimental procedure yields the same outcome.

ANSWER: *T*

44.   In the Spencer and Weisberg experiment, subjects were given two training problems under the
       pretext that all three problems were part of a pilot experiment.

ANSWER: *T*

45.   The power of a statistical test is partially determined by the number of subjects.

ANSWER: *T*

46.   One factor affecting reliability is the number of observations per experimental condition.

ANSWER: *T*

47.   Between-subjects designs tend to produce data that are more variable than data obtained from within-subjects designs.

ANSWER: *T*

48.   Holyoak's theory of structural consistency helps to specify the conditions under which analogous solutions are difficult or easy.

ANSWER: *T*

49.   Gick and Holyoak (1980) found no difference in problem solving performance between subjects who read an analogous problem story prior to solving a problem and subjects who did not.

ANSWER: *F*

50.   Inferential statistics are used to determine whether an experimental outcome would have occurred by chance.

ANSWER: *T*

51.   If an experimental result is real there is no need to repeat it in a conceptual replication.

ANSWER: *F*

52.   If a result is not reliable then it probably will not generalize to other settings.

ANSWER: *T*

53.   Lack of experimental control often leads to high error variance.

ANSWER: *T*

54.   Functional fixity is observed when a common object is used in some novel and creative manner.

ANSWER: *F*

55.   Verbal reports are accepted as dependent measures in psychological research since they are so unreliable.

ANSWER: *F*

56.   It is advisable to use verbal reports in conjunction with other behavioral measures rather than as the sole source of evidence for a phenomenon.

ANSWER: *T*

57.   There is strong evidence that incubation plays an important role in problem solving.

ANSWER: *F*

58.   The key to experimental replicability is the systematic manipulation or control of relevant variables.

ANSWER: *T*

59.   The terms verbal report and subjective report are interchangeable.

ANSWER: *T*

60.   Metcalfe found that the "feeling-of-warmth" ratings that subjects gave as they attempted to solve a problem tended to follow an insight pattern.

ANSWER: *T*

61.   Introspective reports are more common in psychology today than they were in psychology 100 years ago.

ANSWER: *F*

62.   The major important tactic of the General Problem Solver computer program was its strict reliance on a means-end strategy.

ANSWER: *F*

Essay

63.   Discuss similarities and differences between Holyoak's theory of structural consistency and McClelland and Rumelhart's model of word recognition.

64.   Briefly describe the research conducted by Thorndike and Kohler on problem solving. How did these two researchers differ in their approaches to this problem?

65.   Distinguish between experimental and statistical reliability. Which of these is more important and why? How might the failure to replicate a result be an interesting contribution to knowledge about a phenomenon?

66.   Describe Holyoak's model of analogical correspondence between the tumor problem and the fortress problem. Discuss how the model accounts for analogical transfer.

67.   Functional fixity, mental blocks and mental set may hamper the solving of a problem. Explain each of these terms and describe an experiment for each that supports the claim that they can have a negative effect on problem solving.

_____

** Text Page References for Test Questions can be found in Appendix C

Individual Differences and Development

Key Terms

AI (artificial intelligence)
analytical approach
Chinese room
chronological age
cohort
cohort effects
construct validity
cross-sectional design
cross-sequential design
empirical approach
face validity
intelligence
longitudinal design
mental age
multiple intelligences

parallel forms of a test
predictive (criterion) validity
quasi-experimental designs
regression artifact
regression to the mean
reliability
split-half reliability
strong AI
subject variables
test-retest reliability
time-lag design
tonal agnosia
Turing test
validity
weak AI

Answers to Discussion Questions

1. *Reliability refers to the consistency of some measure used to assess a construct. That is, does the dependent variable measure the same thing every time? To the degree that the measure yields the same result across multiple assessments it is said to be reliable. Reliability of a test may be determined in three ways. Test-retest reliability refers to the correlation between successive test scores obtained from a single group of subjects. The higher the correlation the better the reliability of the test. If it is undesirable to repeat specific items from one testing to the next for fear of practice effects and the like, parallel forms of the test may be administered on two separate occasions and their scores correlated. Finally, scores for items from a single test may be correlated with one another using a split-half technique whereby items are arbitrarily divided into two groups for comparison.*

2. *Operational definitions enable psychologists to define precisely the terms of which they speak. This is important since psychologists are often concerned with studying abstract constructs that might otherwise have many semantic interpretations. For instance, one researcher might define aggression in monkeys as the invasion of another's territory whereas another researcher's definition might involve actual physical combat. Thus it is easy to see how these different operational definitions might lead to different conclusions about aggression in monkeys.*
    Operational Definitions:
    a) thirst: number of hours of water deprivation; percent decrease in water intake over a long period
    b) intelligence: percentile score on the SAT; proportion correct on a crossword puzzle task
    c) memory capacity: number of digits correctly repeated after a 20 second retention interval; number of words recalled one week after initial presentation of a list of words d) sexual satisfaction: average number of times a person engages in sex during a one month period; percentile score from a questionnaire concerning sexual satisfaction
    e) fear of snakes: change in GSR when snake presented; average distance voluntarily maintained between subject and snake during a five minute period

3. *a) The cross-sectional design allows the experimenter to readily obtain observations from several groups of subjects of different ages and is the most often used design for studies employing age as an independent variable. Unfortunately, many other factors such as educational level are likely to be*

confounded with age in cross-sectional designs, thus clouding interpretations of experimental results.
b) Many of the problems associated with cross-sectional designs are eliminated in longitudinal studies in which the same subjects are repeatedly tested across time. One disadvantage of longitudinal studies is that their findings might be influenced by historical changes in sociological attitudes and the like. In addition, since these studies are run over extended periods of time it is often difficult for experimenters to keep track of their subject population.
c) Cross-sequential designs incorporate both longitudinal and cross-sectional components into one study by testing subjects born in successive years in later successive years. If both the cross-sectional and longitudinal components of the design show change with age for a dependent variable that is not observed in the time lag component of the design, then the experimenter may conclude that the change is due to age and not to some other confounded factor. The major disadvantage to cross-sequential designs is a practical one involving difficulties inherent in testing the same people over a number of years.

4. *The strong AI approach to intelligence holds that it is necessary for machines to possess a cognitive state that would be called intelligence if a person possessed that cognitive state. From this approach, the manipulation of the fixed symbols in the program would underlie intelligence. The cognitive state that would be called intelligence is realized in the program that runs the machine. In addressing the question of whether computers are intelligent, definitional problems inevitably arise. For example, what does it mean to possess a cognitive state? If one relies on a more concise operational definition of intelligence such as that provided by the Turing test, questions concerning the validity of the definition arise. Searle's hypothetical experiment known as The Chinese Room is one example. If you adopt a pragmatic view and accept that a behavior of a machine that manipulates symbols is intelligence, which is what some consider a strong AI approach, then computers would be described as intelligent.*

5. *The first problem with the pet therapy study is that there is no control group against which to assess change in mental state. Unless it may be determined that the pet group improved differentially in comparison to a similar group of control subjects, there is no logical way to attribute the outcome to the manipulation of the independent variable. That is, it may be the case that the subjects in the study would have become less depressed over the two month period without any treatment. Or it could be that the observed improvement in mental state is a placebo effect which would have been observed for any treatment given to the subjects. Finally, one outcome may have been due to a regression artifact in which measurement error produced scores for some subjects that overestimated depression level on the first testing. Thus, with regression to the mean, the scores for the second testing appear "improved" when in fact no real improvement has taken place.*

6. *In general, this statement is true because subjects are never randomly assigned to groups when subject variables are studied. Since subject variables are not directly controlled by the experimenter, the studies may be considered as quasi-experiments. That is, subject variables may always be confounded with other uncontrolled factors. One way in which to make results from experiments employing subject variables more readily interpretable is to used cross-sequential designs. Since these designs incorporate longitudinal, cross-sectional, and time lag components, the effects of confounded variables such as historical change may be partialled out. The adoption of such designs is crucial since there are an array of subject variables that are theoretically important to psychologists and need to be studied, including age, IQ, sex, education level, socioeconomic status, reading ability, birth order, race, religion, marital status, and weight.*

Lecture Suggestion

Although the topic of reliability was discussed at length in the text, there is another criterion that dependent measures should meet, namely validity. When we say that a measure is valid, we are saying that it measures the hypothetical construct that it was intended to measure. It is important to note that a measure may be reliable without being valid. For instance, repeated administrations of an intelligence test may yield highly similar scores, but the test may not be a valid index of intelligence due to the fact that certain items may be biased in favor of one cultural group or another. As an example, Eells, Davis, Havighurst, Herrick, and Tyler (1951) found evidence of cultural bias for an item requiring children to choose the word that does not belong in this group: cello, harp, drum, violin, guitar. Although the correct answer is "drum", the only instrument without strings, only 45% of the lower-class children answered correctly whereas 85% of students in a higher social class chose the correct answer. Most of the lower-class children who missed the question chose "cello" rather than "drum" since "cello" was a word unfamiliar in their culture whereas the other four items were clearly musical instruments.

In order to illustrate the problem of bias in intelligence testing, it is possible to design tests that are biased in favor of low-income groups (e.g., Aiken, 1971). One such test written by Adrian Dove contains the following items:

*A "Gas Head" is a person who has a: a) fast moving car; b) stable of "lace"; c) "process"; d) habit of stealing cars; e) long jail record for arson.

*Which word is out of place here? a) splib; b) Blood; c) grey; d) Spook; e) Black. (The correct answer is "c" for both items.)

It is not difficult to see how differential cultural learning could affect performance on an intelligence test comprised of biased items and that such tests are certainly not valid. This issue is particularly important since intelligence tests are so often used in selection processes for college admission and hiring in the job market. The area of test bias research should prove to be a very productive one in the near future as we explore the possible implications of validity (or the lack thereof) in testing.

References

Aiken, L.R., Jr. (1971). Psychological and educational testing. New York: Allyn & Bacon.
Eells, K., Davis, A., Havighurst, R.J., Herrick, V.E., & Tyler, R.W. (1951). Intelligence and cultural differences. Chicago: University of Chicago Press.

Demonstration Suggestion

Although all students in the class will have no doubt had experience with some sort of group intelligence test (such as the SAT) most will probably never have seen an individual intelligence test. It would therefore be instructive to divide the class into groups of five or less and let them examine such IQ tests as the Standard-Binet, WAIS, and WISC. See if the students are able to find items which may be considered culturally biased and discuss the implications of the inclusion of these items in the inventories.

Experimental Dilemmas

1.   A researcher interested in measuring people's attitudes toward nuclear power constructed a 60 item attitude scale. For each item subjects were to indicate their agreement or disagreement on a scale of 1 to 5 where a rating of 1 reflected strong agreement and a 5 signified strong disagreement. For instance, a subject in favor of nuclear power as an energy source would be expected to respond with a 5 to a statement such as "The recent proliferation of nuclear power plants poses a serious threat to the safety of the continent." In order to establish the reliability of the scale, the experimenter gave the scale to 50 subjects on two successive occasions with one week intervening between tests and correlated scores from the two separate administrations. A high positive correlation of .75 was obtained. As a further check, the scale was administered to another group of 50 subjects. Before scoring, the

experimenter divided the items in half with equal numbers of statements believed to favor and disfavor nuclear power included in each half. A split-half reliability coefficient of +.86 was obtained when scores from each half of the scale were correlated. Has the experimenter done a reasonable job in establishing the reliability of the attitude scale?

ANSWER: *Yes.*

2. A researcher studying developmental changes in intelligence conducted the following cross-sectional study. The Wechsler Adult Intelligence Scale (WAIS) was administered to subjects of age 20, 30, 40, 50, 60, and 70 years. Twenty subjects were tested in each age group and the following results were obtained.

Age (years)	IQ
20	120
30	110
40	100
50	95
60	93
70	89

From these results the experimenter concluded that IQ peaks early in adulthood and declines steadily thereafter. Do you agree with the experimenter's conclusion? Why or why not?

ANSWER: *No. These results were most likely produced by factors confounded with the age variable. One possibility is that older subjects received less formal schooling than the younger subjects which made their scores appear artificially low. Such confounding could possibly be eliminated in a longitudinal design in which the same subjects are tested over sequential years.*

Questions

Multiple Choice

1. A hypothetical experiment that was devised to assess whether a machine can think is called
    a. the imitation game.
    b. the Chinese Room.
    c. the Turing test.
    d. all of the above

ANSWER: *D*

2. A positive feature of the Turing test is that evaluation of machine intelligence involves
    a. an interrogator.
    b. a multi-factor approach.
    c. an experimental approach.
    d. all of the above

ANSWER: *C*

3.   The primary difference between the analytical and empirical approaches to scientific investigation is that
        a.   empirical approaches attempt to predict events on the basis of theoretical models.
        b.   analytical predictions are based on events accompanying the event of interest.
        c.   analytical approaches are guided by theory.
        d.   empirical approaches provide a deeper understanding of phenomena than do analytical approaches.

ANSWER: *C*

4.   The empirical approach to the study of intelligence
        a.   is concerned with the hypothetical construct of intelligence rather than with scholastic performance.
        b.   primarily involves a search for measures which are highly correlated with school performance.
        c.   is guided by theory.
        d.   is an inductive approach.

ANSWER: *B*

5.   The Turing test provides _____ for artificial intelligence.
        a.   an operational definition
        b.   a hypothetical construct
        c.   a model
        d.   a theory

ANSWER: *A*

6.   A five year old child with a mental age of 10 years has an IQ of
        a.   120
        b.   50
        c.   100
        d.   200

ANSWER: *D*

7.   Psychologists are frequently interested in the degree to which genetic and environmental factors play a role in determining intelligence, so they study twins raised in different homes and compare them with twins reared together. A potential problem with the interpretation of such results is that
        a.   all pairs of children in the same household will not necessarily have equally similar experiences.
        b.   for the twins reared apart, there is a delay between birth and placement in foster homes which may span a critical learning period.
        c.   prenatal experiences are more similar for twins than for other children.
        d.   all of the above.

ANSWER: *D*

8. As _____ increases _____ decreases.
    a. number of observations; reliability
    b. reliability; face validity
    c. measurement error; reliability
    d. stability; reliability

ANSWER: *C*

9. According to Dweck and her associates, children who adopt ____ goals want to look smart and not receive negative evaluations from their peers.
    a. entity
    b. performance
    c. learning
    d. instrumental incremental

ANSWER: *B*

10. An experimenter who gives a test to subjects on one occasion, repeats the test on the same subjects at a later date, and then correlates the scores is interested in _____.
    a. face validity
    b. test-retest reliability
    c. parallel forms reliability
    d. split-half reliability

ANSWER: *B*

11. The main difference between the parallel forms and split- half techniques for assessing reliability is that
    a. the parallel forms techniques involves testing subjects on two separate occasions and the split-half technique does not.
    b. items are arbitrarily divided for comparison in the parallel forms procedure but this is not true for the split-half technique.
    c. a high positive correlation between scores reflects good reliability for the parallel forms procedure but a high negative correlation is indicative of good reliability for the split-half procedure.
    d. split-half correlations reflect stability whereas parallel forms correlations do not.

ANSWER: *A*

12. A theory of multiple intelligences was developed by
    a. Gardner.
    b. Searle.
    c. Turing.
    d. Sternberg.

ANSWER: *A*

13.   Longitudinal studies of intelligence usually show that
    a.   IQ decreases significantly with age.
    b.   IQ increases until middle age and then remains stable.
    c.   IQ is fairly stable from childhood through adulthood.
    d.   IQ is environmentally determined.

ANSWER: *C*

14.   Subject variables
    a.   cannot be experimentally manipulated.
    b.   may be confounded with other factors.
    c.   are never studied in correlational designs.
    d.   both a and b.

ANSWER: *D*

15.   A researcher interested in developmental differences in reading ability, tests three groups of subjects who are either 5, 10, or 15 year old. All subjects are given a test of reading comprehension after reading a fictional passage and scores are compared between groups. This is called a _____ design.
    a.   cross-sectional
    b.   longitudinal
    c.   time lag
    d.   cross-sequential

ANSWER: *A*

16.   Which of the following is true concerning cross-sectional designs?
    a.   They require that the same group of subjects be tested over and over across a long period of time.
    b.   They are much less convenient to run than longitudinal studies.
    c.   They are likely to confound age with some other variable of interest.
    d.   none of the above

ANSWER: *C*

17.   A strength of intelligence tests is that they
    a.   measure one's ability to adapt to new environments.
    b.   predict academic performance.
    c.   have universal validity
    d.   all of the above

ANSWER: *B*

18. The _____ is to Searle, as the _____ is to Turing.
    a. imitation game; Turing test
    b. imitation game; Chinese Room
    c. Chinese Room; imitation game
    d. hypothetical experiment; operational definition

ANSWER: *C*

19. Cross-sequential designs
    a. incorporate features of cross-sectional designs within them.
    b. incorporate features of longitudinal designs within them.
    c. allow the experimenter to attribute changes in the dependent variable to age and not to some other confounded factor.
    d. all of the above.

ANSWER: *D*

20. Quasi-experimental designs are particularly susceptible to bias due to measurement error because
    a. there are no control variables.
    b. subjects are not randomly assigned to groups.
    c. the experimental and control groups are not matched prior to the introduction of the independent variable.
    d. all of the above.

ANSWER: *B*

21. Two students take a History exam. The first student has an A average but makes a C on the test whereas the second student who has a D average makes an A on the exam. Assuming that these discrepancies are due to measurement error, it is likely that the first student will make a(n) _____ and the second student will make a(n) _____ on the next exam.
    a. C; A
    b. A; C
    c. C; C
    d. C; B

ANSWER: *B*

22. Operational definition are usually limited in their _____, which means that they suffer in terms of their _____.
    a. reliability; validity
    b. applicability; reliability
    c. applicability; validity
    d. Operational definitions are not usually limited

ANSWER: *C*

23.   A subject's IQ scores on two separate tests administered two weeks apart were 126 and 120. This
        difference of 6 points is most likely due to
        a.   subject variability.
        b.   measurement error.
        c.   test-retest reliability.
        d.   decline in intelligence level.

ANSWER: *B*

24.   Regression artifacts
        a.   may be avoided with the use of certain experimental manipulations.
        b.   are not a problem when subject variables are being studied.
        c.   are a major problem when subject populations differ.
        d.   occur when the effects of an experimental manipulation subside over time.

ANSWER: *C*

25.   If a test of intelligence is highly correlated with future academic success, the test has
        a.   subjective validity
        b.   predictive validity
        c.   criterion validity
        d.   both b and c

ANSWER: *D*

26.   Sternberg's definition of intelligence emphasizes
        a.   information processing abilities.
        b.   the ability to adopt to new situations.
        c.   the ability for creative thinking.
        d.   all of the above

ANSWER: *D*

27.   The study of individual differences
        a.   has been relatively ignored by experimental psychologists
        b.   began because of important practical decisions that had to be made about people
        c.   is concerned with differences between individual groups in society
        d.   both a and b

ANSWER: *D*

28.   The _____ approach states that it is possible for machines to possess a cognitive state that is
        equivalent to a cognitive state of an intelligent person.
        a.   Turing test
        b.   weak AI
        c.   strong AI
        d.   Chinese Room

ANSWER: *C*

29.   Which of the following is a true independent variable?
        a.   intelligence
        b.   nationality
        c.   age
        d.   none of the above

ANSWER: *D*

30.   Which of the following is a subject variable?
        a.   intelligence
        b.   nationality
        c.   both of the above
        d.   neither of the above

ANSWER: *C*

31.   When a subject variable is studied, it is better to predict _____than _____.
        a.   null findings; main effects
        b.   interactions; main effects
        c.   main effects; interactions
        d.   null findings; interactions

ANSWER: *B*

32.   People with aphasia have a problem with
        a.   self-understanding.
        b.   logical skills.
        c.   spatial skills.
        d.   language.

ANSWER: *D*

33.   The ability of a computer to use programs to model human intelligence is compatible with the
        a.   strong AI approach.
        b.   weak AI approach.
        c.   Sternberg's model of intelligence.
        d.   both a and b

ANSWER: *B*

34.   Operational definitions
        a.   aid communication and understanding
        b.   are best if they are very ambiguous
        c.   are best defined in terms of experimental operations that are used to study them
        d.   both a and c

ANSWER: *D*

35.   Subject variables, by definition,
       a.   can be experimental manipulated in all situations
       b.   are not experimentally manipulated
       c.   are classified as dependent variables
       d.   can be experimentally manipulated in certain controlled conditions

ANSWER: *B*

36.   The Turing test's definition of intelligence has been criticized
       a.   because it is not operational.
       b.   for its lack of validity.
       c.   for its lack of reliability.
       d.   because it does not facilitate communication.

ANSWER: *B*

True-False

37.   The imitation game is called the Turing test.

ANSWER: *T*

38.   Analytical approaches to scientific investigation are guided by theory.

ANSWER: *T*

39.   Empirical approaches provide predictive power whereas analytical approaches do not.

ANSWER: *T*

40.   The empirical approach to intelligence is primarily concerned with predicting school performance.

ANSWER: *T*

41.   The weak AI approach has generated far more controversy than the strong AI approach.

ANSWER: *F*

42.   Intelligence may be operationally defined in terms of school performance.

ANSWER: *T*

43.   Analytical approaches to intelligence have met with greater success in predicting school performance than have empirical approaches.

ANSWER: *F*

44.   IQ scores are obtained using the following equation: (Mental Age/Chronological Age) x 100

ANSWER: *T*

45.   The evaluation of machine intelligence by means of the Turing test involves a correlational approach.

ANSWER: *F*

46.   Fraternal twins are useful as subjects in the study of intelligence because they have the same genetic inheritance.

ANSWER: *F*

47.   An important factor to be controlled in studies of intelligence is specific learning that could affect test performance.

ANSWER: *T*

48.   According to Turing's operational definition of intelligence, we measure intelligence by the amount of deception in the computer's answers.

ANSWER: *T*

49.   If a test in reliable then we know that it measures what it was intended to measure.

ANSWER: *F*

50.   Reliability increases as variability increases.

ANSWER: *F*

51.   The assumption that intelligence remains stable over short periods of time allows us to assess the reliability of intelligence tests.

ANSWER: *T*

52.   Intelligence tests do a good job of predicting academic performance.

ANSWER: *T*

53.   Test-retest reliability involves the administration of one test to two different groups of subjects.

ANSWER: *F*

54.   One way to avoid specific practice effects when assessing the reliability of a test is to use parallel forms of the test.

ANSWER: *T*

55. Subject variables are selected and manipulated.

ANSWER: *F*

56. The split-half technique of assessing reliability involves repeated administrations of the same test.

ANSWER: *F*

57. Longitudinal studies have shown that childhood IQ scores may be used to predict adult IQ scores.

ANSWER: *T*

58. By definition subject variables cannot be experimentally manipulated.

ANSWER: *T*

59. In a cross-sectional research design, the same subjects are repeatedly tested over the course of several years.

ANSWER: *F*

60. The Turing test defines intelligence in such a way that machines could possess intelligence.

ANSWER: *T*

61. Longitudinal and cross-sectional studies often produce different results due to the fact that age may be confounded with other factors in cross-sectional designs.

ANSWER: *T*

62. Regression artifacts are less of a problem when subject populations differ than when subjects are randomly assigned to groups.

ANSWER: *F*

63. Regression artifacts are due to statistical regression rather than to experimental manipulations.

ANSWER: *T*

64. Thus far the empirical approach to intelligence has yielded better predictors of future scholastic performance than has the analytical approach.

ANSWER: *T*

65. Researchers prefer the empirical approach to intelligence because it offers understanding in addition to predictive power.

ANSWER: *F*

66.   In a longitudinal design results may be produced by historical events occurring during the course of the study.

ANSWER: *T*

67.   Psychologists have adopted a standard operational definition of intelligence.

ANSWER: *F*

68.   According to Dweck and her associates, all children adopt performance goals and learning goals.

ANSWER: *F*

Essay

69.   Outline three definitions of intelligence. Describe one weakness and one strength of each definition.

70.   Distinguish between the analytical and empirical approaches to scientific investigation. Is one approach preferable to the other?

71.   Describe an experimental approach to study how the motivational goals of a child influence his or her intellectual performance.

72.   What is reliability? Describe three ways in which the reliability of a measure may be assessed.

73.   Searle argued against the possibility of strong AI. Describe his rationale and a hypothetical experiment that supports his argument.

74.   Briefly describe problems associated with the use of intelligence as a subject variable. How might these problems be avoided?

75.   Research on developmental differences often use longitudinal, cross-sectional and time-lag designs. Explain the differences in these designs and the advantages and disadvantages of each design.

76.   Describe the Turing test and the corresponding definition of intelligence. Are computers intelligent according to this test? Why?

** Text Page References for Test Questions can be found in Appendix C

Social Influence

Key Terms

blind	impact $(I = N^t)$
bystander intervention	obedience
conformity	placebo effect
confounding	randomization
control variables	simulating control subjects
demand characteristics	social facilitation
experimental control	social loafing
experiment error	social norms
experimenter bias	social psychology
field research	

Answers to Discussion Questions

1. *Social situations are generally far more complex than any other type of situation that psychologists might be interested in studying. There are many more covert variables operating to influence outcomes. These factors are often subtle and arise from such uncontrollable phenomena as attitude bias and prior social learning.*

    a) In a bystander intervention study conducted in the laboratory one would want to control variables related to the victim, the bystanders, and the environment itself. For instance the victim's race, age, and type of injury would be controlled if they were not independent variables. These same variables should be controlled for the bystanders in addition to socioeconomic status, education level, sex, and any other number of factors. Certain characteristics of the environment should be controlled such as time of day and length of emergency, whether the accident occurs in a "public" or "private" setting, room temperature, and many others.

    b) While it would be convenient to gain control over all the variables mentioned above in the field setting, it is usually impossible. Although most of the traits of the victim and some of the features of the environment may still be held constant, the traits of the bystanders are more or less left to chance. A judicious choice of the site of the emergency may increase the probability of obtaining bystanders with certain qualities, but there are no guarantees.

2. *The statement taken out of context is usually considered false. That is, if you know that a variable is confounded with another variable of interest and you are able to tease the two apart experimentally, by all means do so. However, it is often the case that isolation of the independent variable from the confounded variable is incredibly difficult, if not impossible. This is often true with subject variables. For instance, some subjects in a study may have more liberal political views than others and these biases may affect the experimental outcome. If, as the experimenter, you have no way to classify subjects on this dimension, the best that you can do is randomly assign subjects to groups in the experiment so that the bias will not vary between conditions.*

3. *Over the long run the falsification of data probably poses no serious threat to the progress of a science. The reason is that if a finding is really important, other scientists will immediately jump on the bandwagon attempting to replicate and extend the result. If the original results are falsified repeated failures to replicate the result will lead to the abandonment of the original line of research. Deliberate fraud is much more detrimental in the short run during which researchers spend their time and energies chasing a red herring when their efforts could have been better spent elsewhere.*

4. *When an experimenter expects a certain result from an experiment, he or she may unwittingly bias the outcome in favor of the hypothesis by subtly communicating these desires to subjects. By the same token, subjects who want to please the experimenter may entertain hypotheses about the desired outcome of the experiment and change their behaviors in accordance with those hypotheses. Both of these biases may lead to artificially produced results which will not generalize to other settings. One way in which to overcome these problems is to run double blind studies in which neither experimenter nor subject know which group is the experimental group or which is the control group. Obviously not all types of research are subject to problems related to demand characteristics of the experimental situation since not all sciences use human subjects. On the other hand, all sciences are subject to experimental bias, although to different degrees.*

5. *The major advantage of field research is that there is no question of whether the results will generalize to real world settings because the studies are conducted in the real world. The problem is that any gain in realism is accompanied by a decline in experimental control.*

6. a) *Laboratory settings:*
    The topic areas of behavioral physiology, perception, and memory are all well suited for laboratory settings primarily because they are most effectively studied with the use of special equipment. It would be almost impossible to gain knowledge in any of these areas without a high degree of experimental control.
    b) *Field settings:*
    Two topics best studied in field settings are the effectiveness of training programs in industry and therapy techniques in clinical work. A program of behavioral change should only be judged in the context for which it was intended, thus field study is essential in these areas. One might also do field work observing the behavior of a particular animal species in its natural habitat rather than bringing the animal into the laboratory where a new environment may produce alterations in behavior.

Lecture Suggestion

The text devotes much attention to bystander intervention (or the lack thereof). The general point was that for various reasons bystanders will often fail to lend aid in some ongoing social emergency. The question may be posed as to how people react to aid from strangers once it is offered. Although we might expect that the response to favors or gifts would be overwhelmingly positive, research has shown that this is not necessarily the case. Gergen, Ellsworth, Maslach, and Seipel (1975) conducted a study in which subjects first suffered heavy losses in a game played with chips. Following the loss, subjects were offered unsolicited aid in the form of extra chips from another (confederate) player. Depending upon the experimental condition, the confederate informed the subject that he expected either no repayment, equal repayment, or repayment exceeding the original donation. Liking for the confederate was subsequently measured. Results showed greatest liking for the confederate asking equal repayment and least liking for the confederate asking extra repayment. Why did subjects like the confederate who asked for no repayment less than the confederate who asked for repayment equal to the gift? Two reasons are offered. First, the norm of social reciprocity is violated when no repayment is required. By this norm people are expected to reciprocate any and all favors. Second, a gift without obligation of repayment may be interpreted as charity, and this induces a negative response in many people.

References

Gergen, K.J., Ellsworth, P., Maslack, C., & Seigel, M. (1975). Obligation, donor resources, and reactions to aid in three cultures. Journal of Personality and Social Psychology, 31, 390-400.

Demonstration

This exercise is intended to demonstrate the power of social norms -- our accepted patterns of behaving and thinking. By the time this chapter is covered, the class will most likely have been in session for several weeks, and students will have established a fixed pattern of seating themselves in the classroom. Without warning, have the seating arrangement changed in the room so that students will be taken by surprise upon entering. For example, if desks are normally lined up in rows have them arranged in a semi-circle. Students will no doubt be taken aback at the change any may even move the desks back into the old pattern in attempts to restore order to the universe. Use the opportunity to discuss our psychological need for rules and norms in even the most trivial of circumstances.

Experimental Dilemmas

1. A researcher interested in group dynamics hypothesizes that if groups of subjects are given a problem to solve, they will be able to reach an unanimous consensus sooner if the group is composed totally of members of the same sex. She proposes the following design. Groups of either six males, six females, or three males and three females will meet in a conference room. The researcher (who will test all of the subjects herself) will give the subjects the resumes of three people who are being considered for a supervisory position in a shipping company. The group's task will be to choose one of the applicants through discussion and deliberation. The experimenter will be present and will act as a moderator but will not attempt to sway the decision one way or another. The amount of time needed to reach a decision will be compared between groups composed of either the same sex or different sexes. Are there any problems in the proposed procedure? If so, what are they?

ANSWER: *It is probably not a good idea for the experimenter to moderate the discussions. Since she knows the hypothesis it is possible that she could communicate her wishes to the subjects through nonverbal communication or by allowing differential amounts of speaking time to subjects with particular views. She should either solicit the services of a moderator who is blind to the experimental hypothesis or dispense with the moderator role altogether.*

2. A researcher investigating the factors responsible for attitude development reported the following study. Groups of five subjects listened to a taped message describing the potential dangers of the trilateral commission. Subjects were either told that the speaker was a high-ranking government official or a local graduate student who had researched the topic. The hypothesis was that attitudes would be more likely to conform to those espoused by the speaker with higher credibility -- the government official in this case. Subjects filled out questionnaires designed to measure their attitudes concerning the trilateral commission both before and after hearing the message. The experimenter who tested the subjects was unaware of the research hypothesis. Subjects were told that the research was conducted in an effort to find out how well informed the general public is concerning political issues. Subjects were led to believe that research was being conducted on several issues, only one of which involved the trilateral commission. Are there any problems with the experimental procedure?

ANSWER: *No.*

Questions

Multiple Choice

1. Latane proposed a theory of social impact that is consistent with the idea that people conform or obey according to a
   a. power function.
   b. multiplicative function.
   c. positive correlation.
   d. negative exponent.

ANSWER: *A*

2. Which of the following topics would <u>least likely</u> fall under the rubric of social psychology?
   a. aggression
   b. reading disabilities
   c. altruistic (helping) behavior
   d. conformity

ANSWER: *B*

3. _____ guarantees that even though a variable cannot be controlled, its influence will not affect the outcome of the experiment by being confounded with the independent variable.
   a. Experiment bias
   b. Randomization
   c. Conformity
   d. A placebo condition

ANSWER: *B*

4. McDougall's view that social behavior is largely determined by instincts
   a. is still the accepted view today.
   b. had very little impact on psychology as a whole.
   c. has since been discredited and abandoned.
   d. stressed the importance of environmental influence.

ANSWER: *C*

5. Sherif studied the impact of social norms on perception using the autokinetic phenomenon and found that
   a. a person's judgments of light movements were greatly determined by reports of other participants.
   b. the light seemed to fade away after several minutes of viewing time.
   c. subjects' reports were unaffected by social norms.
   d. although social norms produce changes in behavior in normal settings, the principle does not extend to perception.

ANSWER: *A*

6.   The autokinetic phenomenon
        a.   occurs when a constant light stimulus appears to blink on and off after extended viewing.
        b.   occurs when a stationary light stimulus appears to move by itself after extended viewing.
        c.   is one perceptual illusion that is unaffected by social norms.
        d.   both b and c.

ANSWER: *B*

7.   A subject will be less likely influenced by a group in a visual discrimination task if
        a.   the group's response is incorrect.
        b.   one member of the group responds correctly.
        c.   the perceptual task is unambiguous.
        d.   all of the above.

ANSWER: *B*

8.   Which of the following is most likely to be used as a dependent variable in a social psychology experiment?
        a.   preference
        b.   reaction time
        c.   percent correct
        d.   spontaneous recovery

ANSWER: *A*

9.   _____ occurs when a change in the dependent variable is produced by some factor other than the change in the independent variable.
        a.   Experimental independence
        b.   Experimental control
        c.   Experimental error
        d.   Randomization

ANSWER: *C*

10.   An experimenter wishes to test the effects of alcohol on driving ability. He has the subjects drink varying amounts of alcohol and then tabulates the number of errors they make on a simulated driving task. In this experiment _____ is the independent variable.
        a.   number of errors on the driving task
        b.   years of driving experience
        c.   amount of alcohol consumed
        d.   reaction time in the driving task

ANSWER: *C*

11. In the experiment described above, _____ is the dependent variable.
    a. number of errors on the driving task
    b. years of driving experience
    c. amount of alcohol consumed
    d. reaction time in the driving task

ANSWER: *A*

12. _____ refers to the finding that patients in medical research who are in a control condition and do not receive actual medication, after show an improvement in the illness.
    a. Conformity
    b. Confounding
    c. The placebo effect
    d. Experimental error

ANSWER: *C*

13. When confounding occurs, the experimenter cannot know whether the independent variable or the second confounded variable produced the change observed on the _____ variable.
    a. extraneous
    b. control
    c. independent
    d. dependent

ANSWER: *D*

14. The teacher-subject's task in the Milgram obedience studies was to

    a. test the learner on a previously presented list of words.
    b. learn a list of paired associates.
    c. increase shock whenever the learner made an error.
    d. both a and c.

ANSWER: *D*

15. In Milgram's obedience studies, the confederate learner
    a. instructed the teacher subject to increase voltage following errors.
    b. was never actually shocked by the teacher subject.
    c. was chosen at random for each experimental session.
    d. only rarely made errors on the memory task.

ANSWER: *B*

16. Experimental control helps to eliminate the problem of
    a. variation in the dependent variable no caused by the independent variable.
    b. experimental error.
    c. interaction effects.
    d. both a and b

ANSWER: *D*

17. Upon testing variations of his original obedience study, Milgram found that
     a. the original subjects had conformed to the experimenter's orders only because the study was conducted at a respected institution.
     b. obedience decreased as the distance between the subject and the learner was increased.
     c. subjects were less likely to shock the learner if he was close by than if he was in another room.
     d. subjects were more likely to shock the learner if other confederate teachers refused to do so.

ANSWER: *C*

18. An experimenter may bias the outcome of a study by
     a. interacting with different groups of subjects in different ways.
     b. nonverbal communication.
     c. deliberately faking the data.
     d. all of the above.

ANSWER: *D*

19. One technique in psychological experiments is to keep the experimenter from knowing the research hypothesis or the experimental condition of the subjects currently being tested. This technique helps to prevent the problem of
     a. demand characteristics.
     b. experimenter bias.
     c. placebo effects.
     d. carryover effects.

ANSWER: *B*

20. Orne and Evans (1965) showed that behavioral compliance effects believed to occur only under hypnosis
     a. could be observed with control subjects.
     b. were probably due to demand characteristics.
     c. could not be replicated.
     d. both a and b.

ANSWER: *D*

21. The field study by Piliavin, Rodin, and Piliavin (1969) on bystander intervention showed that
     a. people were more likely to help an ill victim than a drunk victim.
     b. people were less likely to intervene when a crowd was present.
     c. people were more likely to help a white victim than a black victim.
     d. all of the above.

ANSWER: *A*

22. In Milgram's laboratory studies of obedience, the subject
    a. was forced to obey the teacher
    b. only received experimental credit if he or she obeyed
    c. could leave the experiment at any time
    d. was paid to comply with the experimenter

ANSWER: *C*

23. Social facilitation refers to the phenomenon that
    a. a group of people will often work together to complete a task.
    b. the larger the group, the more the group cooperates.
    c. the smaller the group, the more the group cooperates.
    d. the presence of others can facilitate an individual's performance on a task.

ANSWER: *D*

24. Milgram concluded that Yale University's reputation was not responsible for the high level of compliance because there was _____ between the level of compliance at the university and at a non-university setting.
    a. a significant difference
    b. a numerical difference
    c. no statistical difference
    d. no numerical difference

ANSWER: *C*

25. The problem of _____ is minimized with research in a natural setting.
    a. demand characteristics
    b. confounding
    c. the placebo effect
    d. conformity

ANSWER: *A*

True-False

26. In field research, it is unusually easy to effectively manipulate an independent variable while controlling extraneous variables.

ANSWER: *F*

27. By and large, the topics studied by social psychologists deal with the impact that an individual's behavior has on society.

ANSWER: *F*

28. McDougall's view that behavior is instinctive is still widely accepted.

ANSWER: *F*

29.   Sherif found that judgments of the autokinetic phenomenon were affected by social norms.

ANSWER: *T*

30.   There is an increasing trend for social psychologists to study overt behavior rather than covert preference.

ANSWER: *T*

31.   Experimental control is achieved when there is no way to tell whether some change in behavior is due to the independent variable or to some other factor.

ANSWER: *F*

32.   Confounding occurs when a second variable is intentionally varied along with the independent variable of interest.

ANSWER: *F*

33.   Randomization is one method of reducing experimental error.

ANSWER: *T*

34.   A dependent variable is the behavior measured in an experiment.

ANSWER: *T*

35.   An independent variable is directly manipulated by the experimenter, but a dependent variable is not.

ANSWER: *T*

36.   Social psychological research is in many ways more difficult to perform than other types of psychological research.

ANSWER: *T*

37.   The subjects in Milgram's obedience studies probably did not believe that they were really delivering shocks to the learners.

ANSWER: *F*

38.   Even though Milgram's experimenter had no direct control over the subjects, they still obeyed the experimenter's orders.

ANSWER: *T*

39.   Latane developed a theory of social impact that accounts for obedience and diffusion of responsibility.

ANSWER: *T*

40.   Milgram showed that obedience behavior increased as the victim was brought closer to the subject.

ANSWER: *F*

41.   Results produced by demand characteristics will most likely generalize to other settings.

ANSWER: *F*

42.   Field research is plagued by problems of demand characteristics.

ANSWER: *F*

43.   Laboratory research has shown that bystander intervention behavior is affected by the number of bystanders present.

ANSWER: *T*

44.   Orne and Evan's failure to find a difference between the hypnotized and simulating control subjects provided an alternative explanation of hypnosis.

ANSWER: *T*

45.   If the results of an experiment are produced by demand characteristics of the experimental setting then they may not generalize to other situations.

ANSWER: *T*

46.   Asch's experiments on conformity as evidenced by visual discrimination employed a task where subjects judged which of three lines was closest in length to a standard.

ANSWER: *T*

47.   Field research minimized the problem of experimenter bias.

ANSWER: *F*

48.   Asch's experiments on conformity showed that subjects will conform to the consensus of the group even when their own perceptions tell them otherwise.

ANSWER: *T*

49.   Milgram's obedience studies showed that very few subjects complied with the experimenter's instructions.

ANSWER: *F*

50.   Milgram's obedience studies showed that very few confederates complied with the experimenter's instructions.

ANSWER: *F*

51.   Placebo effects reflect changes in behavior that are due to the manipulation of an independent variable.

ANSWER: *F*

Essay

52.   Outline how the expectation of the experimenter and the subjects can create problems in social psychological research. Indicate ways that the problems can be avoided.

53.   Briefly discuss Milgram's obedience studies. What factors seem to determine whether obedience will occur?

54.   Contrast the findings from laboratory and field research on bystander intervention. What does this tell us about laboratory research?

55.   Describe ways in which the experimental psychologist can reduce the risk of experimental error.

56.   A toy company wants to determine if employees are more productive if they assemble toys in groups or individually. Briefly outline an experiment designed to answer this question. State the null hypothesis, and the independent, dependent and control variables. How could the possibility of demand characteristics and experimental bias be reduced?

57.   Define the following terms and describe how each these potential problems can be avoided.
        (1) demand characteristics
        (2) experimenter bias
        (3) placebo effect
        (4) experimental error

** Text Page References for Test Questions can be found in Appendix C

Environmental Psychology

Chapter Outline

Key Terms

converging operations   informed consent
crowding   personal space
deception   representativeness
density   sample generalization
ethical issues   social pathology
generalization of results   variable representativeness

Answers to Discussion Questions

1. *The two clerics may have tried to argue that it is, in fact, possible to walk on water, since the rabbi had remained dry from his knees up. The scientist would reply to this assertion that the clerics had drawn too broad a conclusion from this empirical test. Specifically the finding that one can "walk on water" holds only under the narrow conditions in which there are solid objects just beneath the surface of the water. Trying to generalize from these narrowly defined conditions to the more general case where there are not objects just below the water's surface would lead to an incorrect conclusion. This example serves to illustrate the problem of variable representativeness.*

2. *One area in which science is not the appropriate path to truth is the area of morality. For example, consider the moral issues involved in the following scenario. A baby is born several months premature. The baby has such severe physical and neurological disorders that it will never be able to live on its own, unassisted by life support systems. The parents and the doctor agree to withhold food from the baby and it dies.*

    The tools of science are irrelevant here, for what possible cause and effect relations are there to be discovered? How could the scientific method ever be applied here? There are any number of other moral issues that are similarly unamenable to study by the scientific method.

    A second area where science is not the appropriate path to truth is that of religion. How could the scientific method be brought to bear upon answering the question of whether or not there is one or more supreme deity? Peoples beliefs in these deities are private and are not subject to public scrutiny, as the scientific method requires.

    It is highly unlikely that the scientific method will be brought to bear upon either of these areas even in the distant future.

3. *Regardless of whether research is applied research or basic research, the same general principles apply to how readily generalizable the results are. There are cases in both applied and basic research in which the results may be readily generalized and other cases in which the results hold only for a narrowly circumscribed set of subjects and conditions.*

4. *There are a variety of potential indices of social pathology. A number of different biological and social-service measures may provide some indication of the "well-being" of a society, although data have not been compiled for all of them. Two biological indices of social pathology for which data are available include mortality rates (infant mortality or standard mortality ratio) and birth rate. Two social-service indices of social pathology include the number of persons under 18 years of age receiving social assistance and the age-adjusted rate of admissions to mental hospitals. Data are available also on these latter two indices.*

5. *One prediction that could be derived from the personal space concept is that people will attempt to move away from someone who invades their personal space. In order to test this hypothesis you might have an experimenter stand in an elevator either very close to another person in the elevator or else far from the*

person in the elevator. If the experimenter remained close to the person in the elevator, then the person might exit the elevator more quickly than when the experimenter stood far away from the other passenger.

This experiment should not be conducted because there might be a great deal of anxiety evoked when the experimenter invaded the passenger's personal space. This could be especially traumatic for a person who was afraid of elevators to begin with. Also, since the passenger would probably try to move away from the experimenter, the experimenter might have to move with the passenger, especially if the elevator ride was fairly long. This could cause additional stress. Finally, it might be possible to test this hypothesis using a less anxiety provoking situation, such as a library or a magazine shop.

6.   *The question as to whether this assignment is ethical or not can only be answered by trying to evaluate the potential risks and benefits from doing the project. The relative risks might be influenced by the type of experiments proposed. An extremely risky proposed project would be rejected by the professor. One that involves less risk, or a more subtle risk factor, might be less likely to elicit a negative reaction from the professor. Also, note that how the professor reacted and was later "debriefed" might influence how potentially harmful the project was.*

Lecture Suggestion

An interesting experiment on the effect of invading another person's personal space was reported by Middlemist, Knowles, and Matter (1976). One problem with studying invasion of personal space is that the experiment typically ends as soon as the invasion occurs. Middlemist et al. overcome this problem by selecting a location for their experiment in which the "subject" had less mobility to escape from the invasion. The location of the Middlemist et al. experiment was a men's restroom, with the subject situated in front of a urinal. Obviously in this situation the subject has relatively little opportunity to leave as soon as another person invades their personal space. This situation thus lends itself to tests of spatial invasion, which is precisely what Middlemist et al. did.

This field study of the effects of an invasion of personal space posed several problems, one of which was the need for a method for unobtrusive observation. The solution to this problem was to construct a new piece of equipment consisting of a periscope concealed in a pile of books. This was placed in a closed toilet stall from which the experimenter was afforded a clear view of the urinals.

Current models of personal space (e.g., Sherrod & Cohen, 1979) relate invasion of personal space to stress. Middlemist et al. used this stress reaction in formulating their dependent variable. Middlemist et al. reasoned that stress should make it difficult to relax the muscles that must be relaxed before urination may commence. Middlemist et al. measured the time interval between when the man stepped up to the urinal and the onset of urination, reasoning that stress would cause this interval to increase. (They also measured another interval, but this dependent variable is sufficient for illustrating the points to be made here.)

Spatial invasion was manipulated by positioning an out-of-order sign and a bucket in either the middle or end urinal in a row of three. A confederate to the experiment occupied one of the two available urinals, leaving the subject only one empty urinal. Depending upon where the confederate and the out-of-order sign were positioned the subject was either adjacent to the confederate or one urinal away.

The results were exactly as predicted. It took longer to commence urination when the confederate was alongside the subject than when the confederate was separated from the subject. This experiment demonstrates that personal-space invasion has rather immediate biological consequences.

References

Middlemist, R. D., Knowles, E.S., & Matter, C.F. (1976). Personal space invasions in the laboratory: Suggestive evidence for arousal. Journal of Personality and Social Psychology, 33, 541-546.

Sherrod, D.R. & Cohen, S. (1979). Density, personal control, and design. In J.R. Aiello & A. Baum (Eds.), <u>Residential crowding and design</u>. New York: Plenum.

Demonstration

The procedure used by Kinzel (1970) may be easily used as a classroom demonstration. One good approach here is to solicit friends of some of the class members to serve as subjects in the demonstration. Variables that might be interesting to examine include the sex of the person whose personal space bubble is being mapped out, the sex of the person approaching, and whether or not the subject comes from a rural or an urban environment. One might hypothesize that, due to the higher population density, urban dwellers might have a smaller personal space than do people from rural environments.

Experimental Dilemma

An academic counsellor was interested in testing the notion that college students do better on mathematics problems when they are freshman than when they are juniors. His hypothesis was that students tend to take more math courses in high school than in college, and as a result their mathematic skills do not improve that much in college.

To test this hypothesis the counsellor persuaded an engineering professor to administer a mathematics achievement test to his freshman engineering class. In order to counterbalance the type of class, the counsellor also tested a class of juniors taking an english literature course. In both classes the dependent variable was the score on the mathematics test.

The results showed that the freshman class scored reliably higher than the junior class on the mathematics achievement test. At first glance the counsellor was a bit sceptical of this result, so he compared the overall high school grade point averages for the students in these two classes. He found that there was no reliable difference in the mean grade point average for these two classes. This indicated to the counsellor that the two groups were in fact comparable in terms of overall academic ability. Hence he concluded that his hypothesis concerning mathematics skills was correct: Freshman do better on mathematics achievement tests than do juniors.

Do you agree or disagree with this conclusion? Why or why not?

ANSWER: *This conclusion should not be accepted because grade (freshman vs. junior) and course (engineering vs. english literature) are completely confounded. Since it is highly likely that in general engineers would have a higher level of mathematics skills than would english majors, it is uncertain whether or not to attribute the observed difference in mathematics test scores to grade or to academic major.*

Questions

Multiple Choice

1.   Science is
        a.   the only path to truth.
        b.   not self-correcting.
        c.   purely inductive.
        d.   able to investigate only certain aspects of human experience.

ANSWER: *D*

2. Which of the following is true concerning the scientific method?
    a. it is self-correcting
    b. it is unlimited in its applicability
    c. it is not the best way to decide which of two opposing beliefs is correct
    d. none of the above

ANSWER: *A*

3. The scientific method is the preferred method of fixing belief because
    a. any other method is invalid
    b. it is self-correcting
    c. it has no limitations
    d. it always provides a definite answer

ANSWER: *B*

4. If density is manipulated by increasing the number of people and holding the room size constant, then any observable differences are best attributed to
    a. density effects
    b. number of people
    c. room size
    d. either or both a and b

ANSWER: *D*

5. Internal states, such as feelings or emotions, are generally measured by
    a. making inferences based upon data obtained from rating scales
    b. direct observation of the subject
    c. physiological measures
    d. all of the above

ANSWER: *C*

6. The right of informed consent
    a. cannot always be granted in research.
    b. is of little concern to psychologists.
    c. is particularly important in correlational studies.
    d. all of the above

ANSWER: *A*

7. Experiments that are representative
    a. serve as good examples of particular research strategies
    b. are generally based upon a totally random sampling procedure
    c. allow us to generalize their results beyond the specific subjects and variables used within the experiment.
    d. are generally based upon within-subject designs

ANSWER: *C*

8.   The question of whether drug X, which has been found harmful to laboratory mice, is harmful to humans is a specific example of the more general problem termed
        a.   sample reliability
        b.   sample generalization
        c.   variable representativeness
        d.   variable generalization

ANSWER: *C*

9.   A marketing company has found that a specific training program works extremely well with the company's top executives. The company now wants to use this program with its middle management personnel, but it is unsure of how successful the program will be. This is a specific instance of the more general problem of
        a.   sample selection
        b.   sample generalization
        c.   sample bias
        d.   statistical reliability

ANSWER: *B*

10.   Many environmental psychologists have turned away from laboratory studies and have turned towards field studies because of
        a.   the problem of establishing variable representativeness in the laboratory
        b.   the greater flexibility for conducting experiments in the field
        c.   the difficulty of conducting well controlled experimental when subjects are aware that they are participating in an experiment
        d.   the difficulty of establishing a physical analog between the real world and the laboratory setting.

ANSWER: *A*

11.   In Calhoun's experiments on the long-term effects of crowding in rats it was shown that
        a.   the strangest behavior observed was that of the adult female rats called "probers".
        b.   female rats often ate their dead infants.
        c.   the mortality rate for the infant rats was highest for infants in the middle pens
        d.   the mortality rate was highest for infant rats in the end pens

ANSWER: *C*

12.   In their study of crowding and social pathology, which of the following after-the-fact statistical techniques did Galle et al. (1972) use to remove the influence of class and ethnicity?
        a.   correlation
        b.   multiple correlation
        c.   partial correlation
        d.   transformation correlation

ANSWER: *C*

13. _____ would be considered a biological index of social pathology.
     a.   Juvenile delinquency rate
     b.   Age-adjusted rate of admissions to mental hospitals
     c.   Standard mortality ratio
     d.   all of the above

ANSWER: *C*

14. The statistical technique of partial correlation is used to
     a.   introduce ex post facto statistical control
     b.   allow definite statements of causation
     c.   increase variable representativeness
     d.   all of the above

ANSWER: *A*

15. Calhoun's studies with rats imply that high density causes pathological behaviors. Galle et al.'s demographic study showed
     a.   that overcrowding causes pathological behaviors in humans
     b.   that overcrowding does not cause pathological behaviors in humans
     c.   there is a correlation relationship between density and social pathology
     d.   there is absolutely no relationship between density and social pathology in humans

ANSWER: *C*

16. In the Saegert et al. (1975) field study on the effects of crowding in humans _____was confounded with _____.
     a.   type of task; density
     b.   time allowed to perform the task; density
     c.   sex of the subject; type of task
     d.   time of day; density

ANSWER: *D*

17. Marshall and Heslin (1975) varied sex of subjects and group size in an experiment that measured the feelings of the subjects towards the group. They found that
     a.   males generally preferred crowded groups regardless of sexual composition of the group
     b.   females preferred crowded groups if they were all females but not if they were of both sexes
     c.   males preferred the mixed sex groups over groups of all males
     d.   both a and c

ANSWER: *D*

18. Prisoners were found to have larger personal space bubbles when they were classified as
     a.   nonviolent
     b.   violent
     c.   depressed
     d.   homosexual

ANSWER: *B*

19.   The technique of using slightly different types of experiments to jointly support a single concept is
        called
        a.   experimental representativeness
        b.   experimental generality
        c.   converging operations
        d.   converging comparisons

ANSWER: *C*

20.   Studies that manipulate independent variables are _____to any correlational study.
        a.   always superior
        b.   never superior
        c.   generally preferred
        d.   both a and c

ANSWER: *C*

21.   Baron and Bell (1976) found that high temperatures do not necessarily lead to increased aggression.
        Generalizing this result to an urban setting, it might be concluded that long hot summers do not
        lead to aggression. This illustrates the general problem of
        a.   incorrect interpretations of the results of a laboratory experiment
        b.   variable representativeness
        c.   subject generalizability
        d.   an inappropriate inference based on data from a flawed experiment.

ANSWER: *B*

True-False

22.   Science typically attempts to focus on a very wide range of questions and avoids ignoring issues
        simply because the questions raised by those issues are difficult to answer.

ANSWER: *F*

23.   In Calhoun's studies on crowding with rats, overcrowding led to higher rates of pregnancy.

ANSWER: *F*

24.   The scientific method is the only way of arriving at the truth, because all other methods can be
        shown to be invalid.

ANSWER: *F*

25.   Measured physical density and perceived psychological density are generally different.

ANSWER: *T*

26.   The basic difficulty with correlational studies is that one can never reach conclusions about causation.

ANSWER: *T*

27.   Galle et al., on the basis of their correlational demographic study of human crowding, were able to find evidence that Calhoun's results concerning overcrowding in rats generalized to humans.

ANSWER: *T*

28.   An independent variable studied by environmental psychologists include density of people.

ANSWER: *T*

29.   A study conducted by Marshall and Heslin (1975) investigated the effects of sex of the group and group size on feelings toward the group. They found that males did not care too much about group size, but females preferred large groups only if the group was of mixed sex and small groups if the group was all female.

ANSWER: *T*

30.   Kinzel (1970) found that violent prisoners have smaller personal space bubbles than nonviolent prisoners.

ANSWER: *F*

31.   Experiments involving deception and concealment must be conducted only with great caution, if at all, because the right of informed consent cannot be granted.

ANSWER: *T*

32.   A criterion that is seldom used for judging the utility of an experiment is its representativeness.

ANSWER: *F*

33.   Baron's (1972) laboratory experiments showed that heat causes aggression.

ANSWER: *F*

34.   One important principle advocated by the American Psychological Association is the right of informed consent.

ANSWER: *T*

35.   The right of informed consent states that the experimenter has a clear obligation to explain to subjects all salient features of the research before the experiment is conducted to allow the subjects the opportunity to decline from participating.

ANSWER: *T*

36.   Statements about causation can only be made if a study has a high degree of variable representativeness.

ANSWER: *F*

37.   Calhoun's studies with rats implied that high density causes pathological behavior.

ANSWER: *T*

38.   Environmental psychologists rarely record feelings and emotion in addition to observable behavior.

ANSWER: *F*

39.   If high density and social pathology showed a partial-correlation coefficient, we would be justified in stating that social pathology is a result of high density.

ANSWER: *F*

Essay

40.   Discuss three studies of crowding and describe how their results might be generalized.

41.   Why have many environmental psychologists begun to turn towards field studies as opposed to laboratory studies? What are the advantages and disadvantages of field studies as compared to laboratory studies?

42.   Why would an experimental psychologist use the technique of converging operations? Describe how the technique has been applied to the study of the concept of personal space.

43.   Define the terms sample generalization and variable representativeness and explain their importance in experimental psychology.

44.   In a correlational demographic study, Galle, Gove and McPherson (1972) studied crowding and social pathology in the city of Chicago. Briefly describe this study in terms of the (1) measures of social pathology, (2) measures of density, (3) statistical technique, and (4) conclusions. Explain why their conclusions should be accepted with caution.

45.   Discuss why the scientific method is viewed as the strongest method of fixing beliefs. Outline potential weaknesses or problems with the scientific method.

** Text Page References for Test Questions can be found in Appendix C

Human Factors

Chapter Outline

Key Terms

dynamic visual acuity   photopic vision
field research   population stereotype
human factors   secondary task
Landolt - C   scotopic vision
large - n design   small - n design
method of limits   subjective measures
objective measures

Answers to Discussion Questions

1. *A variety of ethical issues may arise for the human factors researcher working on a project that has the potential to alter peoples' work environment. The research must consider not only the benefits of changing the environment but also the potential problems that may be created for all individuals. Will the work environment pose a risk to certain individuals (e.g., children) or unfairly discriminate against a certain group of people (elderly)? Although the work environment may improve performance, will working in the environment pose long-term harmful consequences? As with other scientific research (see Chapter 4), human factors research can create ethical concerns. Human factors research involving the environment can potentially improve human life but it may also create hazardous conditions for people.*

2. *The system designer attempts to optimize the human factors of a system. The designer can evaluate potential risks and hazards of the system and alter the system accordingly to minimize or eliminate risks associated with using the system. In addition the designer may consider additional features that do not influence system performance but serve to reduce risk factors. The decisions about safety features are often difficult requiring a balance between costs and benefits.*

3. *Dynamic visual acuity concerns your ability to perceive detail in moving objects. Object color can be an important factor influencing our ability to detect, recognize and perceive detail in moving objects. The benefit r impedance of object color for dynamic visual acuity can depend on a variety of other factors, such as light intensity of the viewing environment.*

    In night viewing conditions, such as with night driving, the color of oncoming cars may affect your dynamic visual acuity. The color of other objects such as pedestrians and emergency vehicles may affect your ability to recognize them. Other situations where object color may be an important aspect of dynamic visual acuity include the many visual displays in our normal life, such as television, movie and computer display screens.

4. *Almost all of the difficulties inherent in field research are the result of lack of experimental control. The researcher cannot generally exert strong control over the environment. Also, it is often times the case that subjects cannot be randomly assigned to conditions. Demand characteristics also represent a serious problem if the subjects become aware that they are in an experiment, although this is less of a problem than in laboratory research where the subject is certain that he is in an experiment.*

    One strategy for combating the problems involved in field research is to use within-subjects designs in which each subject acts as her own control. Another strategy is to try to replicate the study in a number of different settings, in order to be certain that the results will generalize across different situations.

5. *The advantages of studying pilot mental workload in a flight simulator rather than an airplane in flight are related to safety, cost and experimental control: In a flight simulator, mistakes do not endanger lives and equipment. Most flight simulators, relative to airplanes, are less costly to operate and are more*

efficient in terms of time; for example, researchers never have to wait on the weather before operating a flight simulator. Flight simulators allow for more control over the independent, control and dependent variables of interest to the researcher studying pilot mental workload: In the simulator, for example, there is almost unlimited flexibility in manipulating the rate of descent. Flight simulators enable researchers to employ many subjective and dependent measures in situations that would be impossible in an airplane in flight (i.e., at landings and takeoff). Also, simulators provide more control over the experimental situation; for example, a certain flight pattern can be repeated under the same conditions in a flight simulator. The disadvantages of studying pilot mental workload in a flight simulator are related to the question of how well the findings from the fight simulator apply to the in flight airplane. Although the simulator may replicate an airplane in flight extremely well, it is still an artificial environment that differs in some ways from the airplane. Particularly in monitoring mental workload, pilot's may function differently (i.e., attitude differences) on the same task in the fight simulator as compared to the airplane.

Questions

Multiple Choice

1. In a small n design
    a. all subjects must be assigned randomly to experimental and control conditions
    b. the experimental setting is carefully controlled and repeated measures are taken on the dependent variable
    c. inferential statistics are often used to determine the reliability of the results
    d. all of the above

ANSWER: *B*

2. In the term small n design, the n refers to the number of
    a. independent variables
    b. dependent variables
    c. subjects
    d. experimental conditions

ANSWER: *C*

3. The advantage of flight simulators, as compared to airplanes, in conducting aviation research is related to
    a. safety factors
    b. their ability to simulate actual airplane flight conditions
    c. experimental control
    d. all of the above

ANSWER: *D*

4.   As a measure of pilot mental workload, heart rate may be confounded with
        a.   heart-rate variance
        b.   the brain wave index
        c.   physical activity
        d.   the experimental design

ANSWER: *C*

5.   In pilot mental workload research, an objective dependent measure that does not yield statistically
        reliable differences could mean that
        a.   the measure was insensitive to mental workload
        b.   the measure was not measuring mental workload
        c.   the levels of mental workload were too similar
        d.   both a and b

ANSWER: *C*

6.   Objective measures of pilot workload would include a pilot's
        a.   judgment of effort
        b.   heart rate
        c.   response on a questionnaire
        d.   all of the above

ANSWER: *B*

7.   Subjective measures of pilot workload would include a pilot's
        a.   judgment of effort
        b.   heart rate
        c.   response on a questionnaire
        d.   both a and c

ANSWER: *D*

8.   The preference for subjective dependent measures in the study of pilot workload in the field is
        understandable in that
        a.   objective measures often yielded a statistical difference
        b.   subjective measures often yielded a statistical difference
        c.   subjective measures often are influenced by the pilot's expectations about the experiment
        d.   objective measures often are influenced by the pilot's expectations about the experiment

ANSWER: *B*

9.   Which of the following is most likely to provide an objective, continuous and safe measure of
        mental workload?
        a.   a secondary-task technique
        b.   a physiological measure
        c.   a judgment task
        d.   a reaction-time task

ANSWER: *B*

10.   The first commandment of human factors is
        a.   "honor they machine".
        b.   "blessed is technology".
        c.   "honor thy user".
        d.   "complexity is best".

ANSWER: *C*

11.   An important reward for researchers working in the area of human factors is the
        a.   potential to improve human life.
        b.   opportunity to improve equipment safety.
        c.   opportunity to carry out research.
        d.   all of the above

ANSWER: *D*

12.   In human factors research, the most common dependent variable is
        a.   reaction time.
        b.   error rate.
        c.   movement time.
        d.   heart rate.

ANSWER: *B*

13.   In human factors research, a measured component of total time is
        a.   reaction time.
        b.   percent correct.
        c.   movement time.
        d.   both a and c

ANSWER: *D*

14.   Your ability to perceive detail in moving objects is defined as
        a.   dynamic visual acuity.
        b.   static visual acuity.
        c.   photopic vision.
        d.   scotopic vision.

ANSWER: *A*

15.   Visual acuity is often measured by presenting a letter ____, often called a Landolt ____.
        a.   B
        b.   C
        c.   O
        d.   L

ANSWER: *B*

16.   The blue cone system is known to have _____ than other cone systems.
        a.   higher static acuity
        b.   lower static acuity
        c.   higher dynamic acuity
        d.   both a and c

ANSWER: *B*

17.   When you read an eye chart at the optometrist, your _____ is being determined.
        a.   scotopic vision
        b.   photopic vision
        c.   static visual acuity
        d.   dynamic visual acuity

ANSWER: *C*

18.   In general, human factors research involves _____ independent variables as used by
        experimental psychologists.
        a.   the same
        b.   a wider range of
        c.   totally different
        d.   fewer

ANSWER: *B*

19.   A human factors researcher interested in the role of visual illusions in aircraft crashes would use
        similar independent variables as an experimental psychologist studying
        a.   perception.
        b.   memory.
        c.   social psychology.
        d.   environmental psychology.

ANSWER: *A*

20.   In much of applied research, control variables
        a.   are the main concern.
        b.   are easy to control.
        c.   cannot be held constant.
        d.   are examined systematically.

ANSWER: *C*

21.   In night viewing conditions, vision is controlled by the _____ and is called _____ vision.
        a.   cones; scotopic
        b.   cones; photopic
        c.   rods; photopic
        d.   rods; scotopic

ANSWER: *D*

22.   Blue targets are easier to perceive for _____ vision but not for _____ vision.
        a.   scotopic; photopic
        b.   photopic; scotopic
        c.   both scotopic and photopic vision
        d.   neither scotopic and photopic vision

ANSWER: *A*

23.   _____ measures are easier to obtain, whereas _____ measures are easier to verify by researchers.
        a.   independent; dependent
        b.   dependent; independent
        c.   subjective; objective
        d.   objective; subjective

ANSWER: *C*

24.   In human factors research, learned relations and habits common to specific groups are called
        a.   physiological responses.
        b.   population stereotypes.
        c.   traditional stereotypes.
        d.   stimulus-response compatibility relations.

ANSWER: *B*

True-False

25.   The field settings in which most applied research is conducted prevent the kind of experimental control we would demand inside the laboratory.

ANSWER: *T*

26.   In the secondary-task technique, it is important that the secondary task does not change performance on the primary task.

ANSWER: *T*

27.   As a secondary task, the simple probe task was a sensitive measure of pilot workload in the flight simulator.

ANSWER: *F*

28.   A pilot's rating of workload on a scale of 1 to 10 is an important objective dependent measure.

ANSWER: *F*

29.   Rods and cones have similar sensitivities to color.

ANSWER: *F*

30.   Even though the rods cannot recognize color, they still respond with different sensitivity to various wavelengths.

ANSWER: *T*

31.   Faster moving targets are easier to perceive.

ANSWER: *F*

32.   Blue targets are easier to perceive for scotopic vision, but not for photopic vision.

ANSWER: *T*

33.   In many human factor settings, the traditional large - n research methodology cannot be employed.

ANSWER: *T*

34.   In the study of mental workload, subjective measures are easier to verify than are objective measures.

ANSWER: *F*

35.   Population stereotypes are the idiosyncratic habits of a few individuals in a specific population.

ANSWER: *F*

36.   The most common independent variable in human factors research is error rate.

ANSWER: *F*

37.   In practical situations, excessive response time can be equivalent to an error.

ANSWER: *T*

38.   Total time to complete a task can be separated into the components of reaction time and movement time.

ANSWER: *T*

39.   The automobile driver's detection of oncoming traffic requires dynamic visual acuity.

ANSWER: *T*

40.   If the automobile driver is operating the vehicle during the night, photopic vision is particularly important.

ANSWER: *F*

41.   Static acuity is an excellent predictor of dynamic acuity.

ANSWER: *F*

Essay

42.   Why is the small n design a frequently used design in applied psychology? What are the advantages and disadvantages of small n designs?

43.   Describe Long and Garvey's (1988) study of the effect of wavelength (color) upon dynamic visual acuity, including method, independent and dependent variables, and results. What are the practical implications of the findings?

44.   Briefly describe how laboratory research on attention was applied to aviation research outside the laboratory.

45.   Both objective and subjective dependent measures are used in the field research on pilot mental workload. (1) Explain the differences between the two types of measures. (2) List three examples of each type of measure. (3) Describe the advantages and disadvantages of each type of measure.

46.   Define what is meant by human factors. Describe the influence of experimental psychology on human factors research.

47.   Is a physiological measure of pilot mental workload an objective or subjective measure? Explain why. Describe the advantages and disadvantages of this type of measure. List two examples of a physiological measure of pilot mental workload.

** Text Page References for Test Questions can be found in Appendix C

Experimental Psychology: A Historical Sketch

Appendix Outline

Key Terms

affections	psychophysics
behaviorism	radical behaviorism
cognitive psychology	reaction-time experiment
dualism	sensations
Fechner's law	shape constancy
functionalism	stimulus error
Gestalt psychology	structuralism
introspection	Weber's law
just noticeable difference (j.n.d.)	

Questions

Multiple Choice

1. According to the theory called _____, the body is governed by physical laws but the mind is not.
   a. monism
   b. dualism
   c. pluralism
   d. bilingualism

ANSWER: *B*

2. The writings of Descartes
   a. promoted the separation of the mind and body
   b. advanced the idea that the mind and body could interact
   c. advanced the idea that animals could be studied by the methods used in the physical sciences
   d. both a and c

ANSWER: *B*

3. Many of the early German physiologists in the nineteenth century believed that forces in the human were
   a. mental and physical
   b. chemical and physical
   c. mental and chemical
   d. chemical and biological

ANSWER: *B*

4. The British empiricist philosophers included
   a. Locke
   b. Berkeley
   c. Hume
   d. all of the above

ANSWER: *D*

5.   Helmholtz calculated the rate of nervous impulses to be
    a.   close to the speed of light
    b.   faster than the speed of sound
    c.   relatively slow at about 50 meters per second
    d.   very slow at about 10 meters per minute

ANSWER: *C*

6.   In his reaction-time experiments, Helmholtz found _____ in reaction-time in

_____ .
    a.   great variability; the same subject
    b.   little variability; the same subject
    c.   great variability; among subjects
    d.   both a and c

ANSWER: *D*

7.   Who founded the important discipline of psychophysics?
    a.   Weber
    b.   Fechner
    c.   Wundt
    d.   Ebbinghaus

ANSWER: *B*

8.   Wilhelm Wundt has been credited with establishing the
    a.   first laboratory of experimental psychology
    b.   structural school of psychology
    c.   first psychology journal
    d.   all of the above

ANSWER: *D*

9.   Ebbinghaus completed pioneering experiments on
    a.   sensation and perception
    b.   human physiology
    c.   human problem solving
    d.   human learning and memory

ANSWER: *D*

10.   The structuralist school of psychology attempted to understand
    a.   the higher cognitive processes
    b.   the basic elements of mental experience
    c.   the fundamental laws of behavior
    d.   the physiological basis of thought

ANSWER: *B*

11.   Which of the following schools relied predominately on the method of introspection?
       a.   Gestalt
       b.   behaviorist
       c.   functionalist
       d.   structuralist

ANSWER: *D*

12.   Who of the following was a behaviorist?
       a.   John Watson
       b.   John Dewey
       c.   B. F. Skinner
       d.   both a and c

ANSWER: *D*

13.   Which school(s) of psychology began largely as a protest against structuralism?
       a.   Gestalt
       b.   functionalist
       c.   behaviorist
       d.   all of the above

ANSWER: *D*

True-False

14.   Early dualists argued the mind could control the body, but that there was little influence in the opposite direction.

ANSWER: *F*

15.   The British empiricists disagreed with the belief that the mind could be modeled like a physical systems.

ANSWER: *T*

16.   The structuralists are known for their use of the reaction-time experiment.

ANSWER: *F*

17.   Helmholtz found that the reaction-times of a subject varied very little on different trials.

ANSWER: *F*

18.   The jnd increases as the weight of the standard decreases.

ANSWER: *F*

19.   Weber found that the ratio of the amount of difference necessary to produce a jnd to the standard was a constant.

ANSWER: *T*

20.   Wundt did believed that the higher mental processes such as memory and thought could not be studied experimentally.

ANSWER: *T*

21.   The introspective method was common to structuralism and behaviorism.

ANSWER: *F*

22.   The behaviorists argued that terms such as consciousness were not useful scientific constructs.

ANSWER: *T*

23.   Gestalt psychologists argued that perception of objects was simply the sum of the parts.

ANSWER: *F*

24.   Cognitive psychologists study unobservable mental events with objective, scientific methods.

ANSWER: *T*

Essay

25.   What is Weber's Law? Briefly describe the method used by Weber in investigating this law.

26.   List the four main schools of psychology from 1890 to 1940. For each school, state the subject matter, research methods and two prominent names associated with the school.

27.   Briefly describe the contributions of two important persons to early scientific psychology.

_____

** Text Page References for Test Questions can be found in Appendix C

Statistical Reasoning: An Introduction

Key Terms

alpha level	nondirectional test
analysis of variance	nonparametric tests
arithmetic mean	normal curve
average	null hypothesis
between-groups variance	one-tailed test
biased sample	parameters
correlation	parametric tests
correlation coefficient	Pearson r
central tendency	population
degrees of freedom	power of a statistical test
descriptive statistics	qualitative variation
directional test	quantitative variation
dispersion	random sample
distribution of sample means	range
experimental hypothesis	related measures design
F test	reliability
frequency distribution	replacement
frequency polygon	robust tests
gambler's fallacy	sample
histogram	sign test
homogeneity of variance	simple (one-factor) analysis of variance
inferential statistics	sized sign test
inflection point	standard deviation
interaction effect	standard error of the mean
level of confidence (or level of significance)	statistics
limit	t-test
main effect	two-tailed test
Mann-Whitney U test	type-I error
mean	type-II error
mean duration	variance
median	Wilcoxon signed-ranks test
mode	within-groups variance
multifactor analysis of variance	z score (or standard score)

Lecture Suggestion/Sample Problems

The instructor may not wish to require students to master the statistical tests of significance presented in the Appendix. However, students should be made aware then when considering an array of data, measures of dispersion are as important as measures of central tendency. The following example serves to illustrate the importance of considering variance in addition to the mean.

In a football game, running back A gained 10 years of each of 10 carries. In the same game, running back B gained 1 yard on each of 9 carries, and on his tenth carry managed to break loose for a gain of 91 yards. While both players have the same average gain per carry, which played the more consistent game?

In order to give students the opportunity to compute the statistics described in the Appendix, the following problems are provided.

1. A clinical psychologist gave 30 people, chosen at random, a personality test. The following set of numbers is the subjects' extroversion scores. Find the mean, median, and mode of this distribution. Using a class interval of 10, draw a frequency distribution. How would you describe the distribution? Why?

    23 34 42 51 63 74 85 36 44 53 64 76 37 46 55

    66 77 48 55 69 44 55 64 46 56 65 58 57 52 55

    Mode = 55, Median = 55, mean = 55; normal distribution

2. Perform the following experiment. Take a sample of 100 words (at random) from a popular magazine such as Time. Count the number of letters in each word and draw a frequency distribution of the word lengths. Find the mean, median, and mode of this distribution. Do the same for a sample of words from an advanced text and a children book. How do the distributions change?

3. The mean I.Q. of the general population is 100 and the standard deviation is 15. A psychologist randomly selected 25 high school students and found that their mean I.Q. was 105. The psychologist also randomly selected 100 university students and found that their mean I.Q. was also 105. Are both samples random samples from the general population?
    High school sample: z score = 1.67
    University sample: z score = 3.33

4. A psychology instructor wanted to demonstrate that experimenter effects can influence a subject's behavior. In order to show this, the instructor randomly picked 16 students from his class. The instructor gave each student a word association test. For each word the instructor gave, the student had to report the first word that came to mind. During the first 15 minutes of the test the instructor did nothing other than present the words. During the second 15 minutes of the test the instructor nodded each time a student gave an adjective as a response. The instructor had predicted that nodding would reinforce the students and that consequently the students would give more adjectives as responses in the second 15 minutes of the test than in the first 15 minutes. Below are the number of adjectives each student gave in each half of the test. Determine whether the students gave more adjective responses in the second 15 minutes than in the first 15 minutes using (a) the sign test, and (b) the Wilcoxon signed-ranks test.

First 15 Minutes	Second 15 Minutes
20	23
24	28
15	29
23	27
17	28
21	23
22	20
16	21
19	27
24	29
23	20
21	27
25	26
24	23
23	21
18	27

(a) Sign test: p = .038

(b) Wilcoxon: p < .005 (one-tailed test)

5.   A social psychologist believes that watching violent TV shows makes young children more violent. In order to test this idea, the psychologist showed one group of children a violent movie and another group of young children a nonviolent movie. After watching the movie the children were allowed to play. The psychologist counted the number of aggressive acts of each child during play. Below are the counts for each child in each group. Determine whether the children who watched the violent movie engaged in more aggressive behavior by using (a) the Mann-Whitney U test and (b) the one-factor ANOVA.

Non-Violent Movie	Violent Movie
4	11
7	10
1	10
8	4
4	8
2	6
8	2
9	5
0	2
6	12
3	13
4	10
7	7
0	7
6	6

(a) Mann-Whitney U test:
   U = 164.5
   U' = 60.5 p < .025 (one-tailed test)
(b) ANOVA:

SOURCE	df	SS	MS	F	P
Between-groups	1	64.54	64.54	6.25	<.025
Within-groups	28	289.33	10.33		
Total	29	353.87			

Questions

Multiple Choice

1. The two properties about a set of measurements of a dependent variable that we are most interested in describing are
    a. frequency and average
    b. average and correlation
    c. central tendency and dispersion
    d. histograms and polygons

ANSWER: *C*

2. A frequency polygon
    a. shows what x score goes with a particular value of y
    b. shows how frequently particular scores occurred
    c. can be formed by joining the midpoints of the bars in a histogram
    d. all of the above
    e. both b and c

ANSWER: *E*

3. The _____ is the sum of all the scores divided by the number of scores
    a. median
    b. mean
    c. mode
    d. standard deviation

ANSWER: *B*

4. The generally preferred measure of central tendency is usually the
    a. range
    b. mean
    c. standard deviation
    d. median
    e. standard score

ANSWER: *B*

5.   The mean is
        a.   the arithmetic average
        b.   the middle score
        c.   the average of the highest and lowest scores
        d.   the most common score
        e.   both b and c

ANSWER: *A*

6.   The _____ divides a distribution in half.
        a.   range
        b.   mean
        c.   mode
        d.   median

ANSWER: *D*

7.   An advantage of the median over the mean is that the median is
        a.   easier to calculate
        b.   more sensitive to each of the sample scores
        c.   a measure of dispersion
        d.   less influenced by extreme scores
        e.   often found between the limits of a score

ANSWER: *D*

8.   The mode is
        a.   the arithmetic average
        b.   the middle score
        c.   the most frequent score
        d.   the least frequent score
        e.   the standard score

ANSWER: *C*

9.   Which of the following is the most useful descriptive statistic for measuring dispersion?
        a.   range
        b.   variance
        c.   mean deviation
        d.   standard deviation

ANSWER: *D*

10. The variance of a group of scores is just like the absolute mean deviation except that for the variance
     a. the absolute value of the differences is used instead of the squared value
     b. the squared value of the differences is used instead of the absolute value
     c. differences are based on the median instead of the mean
     d. differences are based on the mean instead of the median
     e. both b and d

ANSWER: *B*

11. The standard deviation is
     a. the square of the variance
     b. the square root of the variance
     c. smaller than the mean
     d. a measure of dispersion
     e. both b and d

ANSWER: *D*

12. The difference between the standard deviation and the variance is
     a. the variance is bigger when the standard deviation is greater than 1.0
     b. the standard deviation is used for description, while the variance is more important for inferential statistics
     c. the variance measures dispersion, while the standard deviation measures central tendency
     d. all of the above
     e. both a and b

ANSWER: *A*

13. All of the following statements are true of the normal distribution except
     a. the mean, median, and mode coincide
     b. the most common scores lie near the mean
     c. the more rare the score is, the further from the mean it lies
     d. the right half of the curve is a mirror image of the left half
     e. nearly all the scores lie outside of two standard deviations

ANSWER: *E*

14. A score that lies one standard deviation above the mean
     a. has the same X value as the point of inflection
     b. has a z-value of 1.0
     c. is no more or less unusual than a score that lies one standard deviation below the mean
     d. all of the above
     e. both a and b

ANSWER: *D*

15.   If the mean I.Q. is 100 and the standard deviation of I.Q. scores is 15, then an I.Q. of 130 will have
        a z score (or standard score) of
        a.   1.00
        b.   0.00
        c.   2.00
        d.   -2.00

ANSWER: *C*

16.   Inferential statistics allow you to decide whether a difference between the experimental and the
        control group is due to _____ or _____.
        a.   manipulation; chance
        b.   manipulation; experimental error
        c.   sampling error; independent variable
        d.   independent variable; experimental error
        e.   chance; experimental error

ANSWER: *A*

17.   A sample is to a population as a _____ is to a _____.
        a.   statistic; parameter
        b.   description; inference
        c.   statistic; inference
        d.   fact; datum
        e.   mean; standard error of the mean

ANSWER: *A*

18.   In order for us to generalize from the sample to the population, it is important that the sample be
        a.   random
        b.   large
        c.   representative
        d.   reliable
        e.   all of the above

ANSWER: *E*

19.   As the size of the sample increases, the _____ of the distribution of sample means
        becomes _____.
        a.   mean; larger
        b.   mean; smaller
        c.   standard deviation; larger
        d.   standard deviation; smaller
        e.   both a and d

ANSWER: *D*

20. The null hypothesis suggests that the two samples come from _____ distribution(s), and the experimental hypothesis suggests that the two samples come from _____ distribution(s).
    a. different; different
    b. different; the same
    c. the same; different
    d. the same; the same

ANSWER: *C*

21. In comparison with a confidence level of 0.05, a confidence level of 0.01 means
    a. you are less sure that the null hypothesis is wrong
    b. you are more sure that the null hypothesis is wrong
    c. you are absolutely sure that the null hypothesis is wrong
    d. you are more sure that the experimental hypothesis is wrong

ANSWER: *B*

22. Rejecting the null hypothesis when it is actually false is
    a. a type I error
    b. a type II error
    c. more likely with two-tailed tests
    d. an error of commission
    e. a correct decision

ANSWER: *E*

23. Failing to reject the null hypothesis when it is actually true is a
    a. type I error
    b. type II error
    c. reasonable thing to do
    d. result of an inappropriate level of confidence

ANSWER: *C*

24. Failing to reject the null hypothesis when it is actually false is a
    a. Type I error
    b. Type II error
    c. standard error
    d. silly thing to do

ANSWER: *B*

25.   As the level or p-level we employ in determining statistical significance decreases (e.g., from .05 to .01), the probability of making a Type I error _____ and the probability of making a Type II error _____.
       a.   increases; increases
       b.   decreases; decreases
       c.   increases; decreases
       d.   decreases; increases

ANSWER: *D*

26.   A conservative statistical test is one that
       a.   minimizes both type I and type II errors
       b.   minimizes type I errors, but increases the chance of type II errors
       c.   minimizes type II errors, but increases the chance of type I errors
       d.   increases the chance of both type I and type II errors
       e.   none of the above; conservative tests have nothing to do with type I or type II errors

ANSWER: *B*

27.   As the sample size (n) increases,
       a.   the standard error of the mean decreases
       b.   the power of the statistical test increases
       c.   the probability of a Type II error decreases
       d.   all of the above

ANSWER: *D*

28.   The power of a statistical test refers to its ability to
       a.   reject false null hypotheses
       b.   reject false experimental hypotheses
       c.   reject true null hypotheses
       d.   reject true experimental hypotheses

ANSWER: *A*

29.   The larger the sample, the more we can trust the sample _____ to be an estimate of the population _____.
       a.   mean; mean
       b.   standard error of the mean; standard deviation
       c.   standard error of the mean; variance
       d.   difference; mean
       e.   both b and d

ANSWER: *A*

30.   In comparison with one-tailed tests, two-tailed tests are
       a.   more powerful
       b.   less powerful
       c.   more conservative
       d.   less conservative
       e.   both b and c

ANSWER: *E*

31.   The Mann-Whitney U test is
       a.   nonparametric
       b.   distribution free
       c.   designed for two groups of scores
       d.   intended for use in between-subjects designs
       e.   all of the above

ANSWER: *E*

32.   The Wilcoxon signed-ranks test
       a.   cannot be used for between-subject designs
       b.   takes into account both the magnitude and the direction of the difference between paired
             scores
       c.   is more powerful than the sign test
       d.   all of the above

ANSWER: *D*

33.   The F statistic is
       a.   a ratio of two independent, unbiased estimates of the population variance
       b.   between-groups variance minus within-groups variance
       c.   within-groups variance minus between-groups variance
       d.   both a and c

ANSWER: *A*

34.   If experimental treatments produce an effect,
       a.   between-groups variance will increase
       b.   between-groups variance will decrease
       c.   within-groups variance will increase
       d.   within-groups variance will decrease

ANSWER: *A*

35.   In a multifactor analysis of variance, how the variables affect one another are called
       a.   main effects
       b.   interaction effects
       c.   experimental effects
       d.   variance effects

ANSWER: *B*

36.   Simple analysis of variance is used in designs having
        a.   one independent variable
        b.   more than one independent variable
        c.   one dependent variable
        d.   more than one dependent variable

ANSWER: *A*

37.   Which of the following are parametric tests?
        a.   Mann-Whitney U Test
        b.   sign test
        c.   t test
        d.   all of the above
        e.   none of the above

ANSWER: *C*

38.   The Pearson product-moment correlation coefficient is referred to as
        a.   z-score
        b.   s.d.
        c.   r
        d.   p.c.c.

ANSWER: *C*

39.   In hypothesis testing, both the magnitude of the difference and the direction of the difference
        between two groups are considered in
        a.   two-tailed tests
        b.   one-tailed tests
        c.   parametric tests
        d.   nonparametric tests

ANSWER: *A*

40.   The inflection point in the normal curve is _____ from the mean.
        a.   less one standard deviation
        b.   two standard deviations
        c.   three standard deviations
        d.   one standard deviation

ANSWER: *D*

True-False

41.   In a histogram the dependent variable is displayed on the ordinate (Y-axis) and the frequency with
        which each value of the dependent value occurred is displayed on the abscissa (X-axis).

ANSWER: *T*

42.   The mode is the measure corresponding to the middle score of a ranked set of scores.

ANSWER: *F*

43.   The primary reason the median is used is that it is insensitive to extreme scores.

ANSWER: *T*

44.   The variance is most useful as a descriptive statistic while the standard deviation of a distribution is used in inferential statistics.

ANSWER: *F*

45.   The variance of a distribution is defined as the sum of the absolute deviations from the mean divided by the number of scores.

ANSWER: *F*

46.   In describing an array of data, psychologists typically present two descriptive statistics, the mean and the variance.

ANSWER: *F*

47.   It is appropriate to compare scores across normal distributions with different means and variances by converting the scores to standard scores or z scores.

ANSWER: *T*

48.   Inferential statistics are used to assess the importance of experimental results.

ANSWER: *T*

49.   Characteristics of a population of scores are called parameters, while characteristics of a sample of scores drawn from a larger population are called statistics.

ANSWER: *T*

50.   If an experiment involving an experimental group and a control group was performed over and over and the distribution of the difference between the means of the experimental and control groups was plotted, this distribution would approximate a normal distribution.

ANSWER: *T*

51.   The standard error of the mean is the standard deviation of a distribution of sample means.

ANSWER: *T*

52.   The standard error of the mean increases with increasing sample size.

ANSWER: *F*

53.   Most hypothesis testing is performed using known population parameters.

ANSWER: *F*

54.   The lower the level or p level we employ in determining statistical significance, the less chance we have of making a Type I error and the greater chance we have of making a Type II error.

ANSWER: *T*

55.   As the level of significance is changed from .01 to .05, the probability of making a type I error increases and the probability of making a type II error decreases.

ANSWER: *T*

56.   The power of a test is the probability of rejecting the null hypothesis when it is actually true.

ANSWER: *F*

57.   Two-tailed tests are more liberal and less powerful than one-tailed tests.

ANSWER: *F*

58.   The Mann-Whitney U test can only be used for between- subject designs and the Wilcoxon signed-ranks test can only be used for related measures designs.

ANSWER: *T*

59.   The variance of a distribution is defined as the sum of the absolute deviations from the mean divided by the number of scores.

ANSWER: *F*

60.   The variance of a distribution is defined as the sum of the squared deviations from the mean divided by the number of scores.

ANSWER: *T*

61.   Approximately 68 percent of the scores in a normal distribution have z values between -2.0 and +2.0?

ANSWER: *F*

62.   Approximately 96 percent of the scores in a normal distribution have z values between -2.0 and +2.0?

ANSWER: *T*

63.   Characteristics of a population of scores are called statistics, while characteristics of a sample of scores drawn from a larger population are called parameters.

ANSWER: *F*

64.   The standard error of the mean is the square root of the mean.

ANSWER: *F*

65.   The standard error of the mean is the mean of a distribution of sample means.

ANSWER: *F*

66.   The standard error of the mean is the variance of a distribution of sample means.

ANSWER: *F*

Essay

67.   What are the difference between inferential statistics and descriptive statistics? Give two examples of each type.

68.   What are standard scores? How are they calculated? Why are they useful?

69.   Why should one try to maximize the sample size?

70.   What are the differences between parametric and nonparametric tests? Give two examples of each type.

71.   Describe three ways that statistics can be misused to create a false impression.

** Text Page References for Test Questions can be found in Appendix C

Text Page References for Test Questions

Chapter 1

1 - p. 3
2 - p. 6
3 - p. 6
4 - p. 7
5 - p. 8
6 - pp. 9-10
7 - pp. 9-10
8 - p. 8
9 - p. 13
10 - p. 10
11 - p. 14
12 - pp. 15-16
13 - pp. 15-16
14 - pp. 10-11
15 - p. 17

16 - p. 17
17 - p. 17
18 - p. 17
19 - p. 20
20 - pp. 20-21
21 - p. 21
22 - p. 8
23 - pp. 9-10
24 - pp. 9-10
25 - pp. 12-13
26 - pp. 8-9
27 - p. 6
28 - pp. 15-16
29 - p. 6
30 - p. 8

31 - p. 10
32 - p. 8
33 - p. 9
34 - p. 7
35 - p. 9
36 - p. 14
37 - pp. 9-10
38 - pp. 14-16
39 - pp. 9-10
40 - pp. 10-11
41 - pp. 12-13
42 - p. 14
43 - p. 8
44 - pp. 14-15
45 - pp. 21-22

Chapter 2

1 - pp. 27-29
2 - p. 26
3 - pp. 26-27
4 - pp. 32-33
5 - pp. 26-27
6 - pp. 32-34
7 - p. 39
8 - pp. 34-35
9 - pp. 40-41
10 - p. 41
11 - pp. 42-43
12 - p. 43
13 - pp. 26-28
14 - pp. 44-45
15 - pp. 39-40
16 - pp. 42-43
17 - p. 39

18 - pp. 44-45
19 - p. 39
20 - pp. 39-40
21 - pp. 46-47
22 - pp. 32-34
23 - pp. 42-44
24 - pp. 27-28
25 - pp. 48-49
26 - pp. 27-29
27 - pp. 39-42
28 - pp. 40-42
29 - pp. 29-30
30 - pp. 48-49
31 - pp. 27-28
32 - pp. 29-30
33 - pp. 34-35
34 - pp. 48-49

35 - p. 37
36 - pp. 48-49
37 - pp. 29-30
38 - pp. 34-35
39 - p. 39
40 - pp. 27-29
41 - pp 41
42 - pp. 41-42
43 - p. 40
44 - pp. 41-42
45 - p. 42
46 - p. 48
47 - pp. 41-42
48 - pp. 42-43
49 - pp. 46-47
50 - p. 42

Chapter 3

1 - pp. 58-59
2 - p. 68
3 - p. 58
4 - p. 58
5 - p. 58
6 - pp. 58-59
7 - p. 59
8 - p. 59
9 - pp. 57-59
10 - pp. 62-63
11 - p. 69
12 - p. 62
13 - p. 70
14 - p. 68
15 - p. 57
16 - pp. 69-70
17 - p. 68

18 - p. 70
19 - p. 71
20 - p. 71
21 - p. 73
22 - p. 56
23 - pp. 58-59
24 - p. 78
25 - p. 75
26 - p. 77
27 - p. 71
28 - p. 66
29 - pp. 72-73
30 - p. 58
31 - p. 66
32 - p. 59
33 - p. 59
34 - p. 58

35 - pp. 55-56
36 - p. 59
37 - p. 58
38 - p. 59
39 - p. 68
40 - p. 59
41 - p. 62
42 - p. 68
43 - pp. 57-61
44 - p. 68
45 - p. 59
46 - p. 65
47 - p. 70
48 - pp. 74-75
49 - p. 83
50 - p. 75

Chapter 4

1 - p. 93
2 - pp. 93-94
3 - p. 98
4 - p. 98-99
5 - p. 102
6 - p. 103
7 - pp. 90-91
8 - p. 91
9 - p. 91-92

10 - p. 93-96
11 - p. 89
12 - pp. 104-105
13 - pp. 93-94
14 - p. 91
15 - pp. 96-97
16 - p. 95
17 - p. 94
18 - p. 95

19 - p. 95
20 - pp. 95-96
21 - pp. 102-103
22 - p. 89
23 - p. 104
24 - p. 91
25 - pp. 93-94

Chapter 5

1 - p. 125
2 - p. 125
3 - pp. 148-149
4 - p. 108
5 - pp. 147-148
6 - p. 108
7 - p. 108
8 - p. 109
9 - p. 109
10 - pp. 111-112
11 - p. 147
12 - pp. 110-111
13 - pp. 110-112
14 - pp. 111-112
15 - p. 112

16 - p. 112
17 - p. 113
18 - p. 110
19 - pp. 109-110
20 - pp. 109-110
21 - pp. 109-110
22 - p. 125
23 - pp. 108, 148
24 - p. 108
25 - p. 109
26 - p. 125
27 - p. 125
28 - p. 125
29 - pp. 109, 125
30 - p. 114

31 - p. 148
32 - p. 108
33 - pp. 109, 113
34 - pp. 110-112
35 - p. 112
36 - pp. 125-126
37 - p. 114
38 - pp. 114-115
39 - p. 125
40 - pp. 147-149
41 - p. 112
42 - p. 110
43 - p. 148
44 - pp. 125, 141
45 - p. 108

Chapter 6

1 - p. 160
2 - p. 159
3 - p. 164
4 - p. 165
5 - p. 159
6 - p. 164
7 - p. 161
8 - p. 160
9 - p. 160
10 - p. 160
11 - pp. 162-163
12 - pp. 162-163
13 - p. 165
14 - p. 165
15 - pp. 166-167
16 - p. 169
17 - p. 170
18 - p. 170-171

19 - p. 159
20 - p. 169
21 - p. 169
22 - p. 171
23 - p. 171
24 - p. 171
25 - p. 169
26 - p. 169
27 - p. 170
28 - p. 176
29 - p. 178
30 - p. 179
31 - p. 180
32 - p. 169
33 - p. 166
34 - p. 163
35 - p. 169
36 - p. 176

37 - pp. 159-160
38 - p. 176
39 - p. 160
40 - pp. 160-161
41 - p. 163
42 - p. 165
43 - pp. 159-160
44 - p. 166
45 - p. 168
46 - p. 169
47 - p. 176
48 - p. 164
49 - p. 176
50 - p. 169
51 - p. 165
52 - p. 165
53 - p. 179

Chapter 7

1 - p. 214
2 - p. 170
3 - p. 189
4 - p. 192
5 - p. 190
6 - p. 190
7 - p. 189
8 - p. 190
9 - p. 197
10 - p. 203
11 - p. 197
12 - p. 204
13 - pp. 204-205
14 - p. 205
15 - pp. 188-189
16 - p. 199
17 - p. 197

18 - p. 210
19 - p. 208
20 - p. 197
21 - p. 207
22 - p. 207
23 - p. 208
24 - p. 211
25 - p. 212
26 - p. 214
27 - p. 190
28 - pp. 204-205
29 - p. 218
30 - p. 189
31 - pp. 190-191
32 - p. 199
33 - p. 215
34 - p. 190

35 - p. 195
36 - p. 204
37 - p. 214
38 - pp. 204-205
39 - pp. 204-205
40 - pp. 188-189
41 - pp. 204-205
42 - pp. 204-205
43 - p. 189
44 - p. 198
45 - pp. 213-214
46 - p. 207
47 - pp. 213-214
48 - p. 208
49 - pp. 219-220
50 - p. 215

Chapter 8

1 - pp. 238-239
2 - p. 235
3 - pp. 234-235
4 - p. 240
5 - p. 227
6 - p. 241
7 - pp. 228-230
8 - pp. 228-230
9 - p. 231
10 - p. 247
11 - p. 231
12 - p. 230
13 - p. 234
14 - p. 231
15 - p. 235
16 - p. 235

17 - pp. 235-237
18 - pp. 235-236
19 - p. 238
20 - p. 238
21 - p. 241
22 - p. 242
23 - p. 235
24 - p. 242
25 - pp. 244-245
26 - p. 244
27 - p. 245
28 - p. 242
29 - pp. 231-232
30 - p. 235
31 - pp. 229-230
32 - p. 230

33 - p. 235
34 - pp. 239-240
35 - p. 241
36 - p. 228
37 - p. 229
38 - pp. 237-238
39 - p. 228
40 - p. 237
41 - p. 243
42 - pp. 244-245
43 - p. 235
44 - p. 242
45 - pp. 226-228
46 - p. 244
47 - p. 246
48 - p. 247

Chapter 9

1 - p. 259	18 - p. 259	35 - p. 259
2 - p. 256	19 - p. 263	36 - p. 257
3 - p. 258	20 - p. 264	37 - pp. 261-262
4 - p. 257	21 - p. 266	38 - pp. 261-262
5 - p. 257	22 - p. 264	39 - p. 283
6 - p. 257	23 - p. 264	40 - p. 265
7 - p. 257	24 - p. 264	41 - p. 258
8 - p. 257	25 - pp. 264-265	42 - p. 264
9 - p. 258	26 - p. 266	43 - p. 265
10 - p. 260	27 - pp. 260-261	44 - p. 264
11 - p. 260	28 - p. 271	45 - p. 266
12 - p. 260	29 - p. 274	46 - pp. 283-284
13 - p. 259	30 - p. 271	47 - p. 275
14 - p. 259	31 - p. 258	48 - p. 256
15 - p. 262	32 - pp. 283-285	49 - pp. 275-276
16 - pp. 261-262	33 - p. 257	50 - p. 258
17 - p. 262	34 - pp. 261-262	51 - p. 259

Chapter 10

1 - p. 316	23 - p. 324	45 - p. 298
2 - p. 295	24 - p. 329	46 - p. 307
3 - p. 298	25 - p. 308	47 - p. 303
4 - p. 295	26 - p. 329	48 - p. 296
5 - p. 297	27 - p. 309	49 - p. 304
6 - p. 296	28 - p. 315	50 - p. 318
7 - pp. 296-297	29 - p. 309	51 - p. 306
8 - p. 298	30 - pp. 315-316	52 - p. 315
9 - pp. 297-298	31 - p. 316	53 - p. 295
10 - p. 299	32 - p. 316	54 - p. 301
11 - p. 299	33 - p. 316	55 - p. 296
12 - p. 298	34 - p. 312	56 - p. 297
13 - p. 301	35 - p. 317	57 - p. 312
14 - pp. 301-303	36 - p. 314	58 - p. 322
15 - p. 299	37 - p. 307	59 - p. 306
16 - p. 300	38 - pp. 315,318	60 - p. 318
17 - p. 300	39 - p. 319	61 - p. 318
18 - pp. 300-301	40 - p. 333	62 - p. 326
19 - pp. 304-305	41 - pp. 315-316	63 - p. 321
20 - p. 302	42 - p. 313	64 - p. 326
21 - p. 307	43 - p. 296	65 - p. 326
22 - p. 324	44 - p. 296	66 - p. 326

Chapter 11

1 - p. 339
2 - p. 345
3 - p. 339
4 - pp. 339-340
5 - p. 340
6 - p. 351
7 - p. 340
8 - pp. 339-343
9 - p. 344
10 - pp. 342-343
11 - p. 346
12 - p. 352
13 - pp. 348-349
14 - p. 347
15 - p. 348
16 - p. 370
17 - p. 348
18 - p. 353
19 - p. 353
20 - p. 370
21 - pp. 353-354

22 - p. 354
23 - pp. 355-356
24 - pp. 359-361
25 - p. 359
26 - p. 348
27 - p. 353
28 - pp. 342-343
29 - pp. 341-342
30 - p. 348
31 - pp. 349-350
32 - p. 350
33 - p. 350
34 - p. 353
35 - pp. 361-362
36 - pp. 370-371
37 - p. 339
38 - p. 339
39 - p. 340
40 - pp. 339-341
41 - pp. 358-359
42 - pp. 342-343

43 - pp. 343-344
44 - pp. 349-350
45 - p. 344
46 - p. 344
47 - p. 344
48 - p. 352
49 - pp. 348-349
50 - p. 347
51 - p. 348
52 - pp. 348-349
53 - p. 353
54 - pp. 353-354
55 - pp. 358-360
56 - pp. 358-360
57 - pp. 364-365
58 - p. 344
59 - p. 358
60 - pp. 361-362
61 - pp. 358-359
62 - p. 370

Chapter 12

1 - pp. 386-387
2 - pp. 387-388
3 - pp. 374-375
4 - p. 375
5 - pp. 387-388
6 - p. 377
7 - p. 378
8 - p. 375
9 - p. 399
10 - pp. 380-381
11 - p. 381
12 - p. 391
13 - p. 383
14 - p. 393
15 - pp. 385-386
16 - pp. 385-386
17 - p. 390
18 - p. 389
19 - pp. 385-386
20 - p. 393
21 - pp. 395-396
22 - p. 375
23 - pp. 380-381

24 - pp. 395-396
25 - p. 388
26 - p. 392
27 - p. 373
28 - p. 388
29 - pp. 378,393
30 - p. 393
31 - pp. 394-395
32 - p. 391
33 - pp. 387-388
34 - p. 375
35 - p. 393
36 - p. 388
37 - pp. 387-388
38 - p. 376
39 - p. 375
40 - p. 390
41 - p. 388
42 - p. 388
43 - p. 376
44 - p. 377
45 - pp. 387-388
46 - p. 378

47 - pp. 382-383
48 - pp. 387-388
49 - p. 375
50 - p. 375
51 - pp. 380-381
52 - p. 390
53 - p. 381
54 - p. 381
55 - p. 393
56 - p. 381
57 - p. 383
58 - p. 393
59 - pp. 385-386
60 - pp. 387-388
61 - pp. 383-384
62 - pp. 395-396
63 - pp. 395-396
64 - p. 390
65 - p. 390
66 - p. 383
67 - pp. 391-392
68 - p. 399

Chapter 13

1 - p. 347
2 - pp. 409-410
3 - p. 417
4 - p. 411
5 - p. 412
6 - p. 412
7 - pp. 412-413
8 - pp. 414-415
9 - p. 416
10 - p. 415
11 - p. 415
12 - p. 426
13 - p. 416
14 - p. 418
15 - p. 419
16 - p. 415
17 - p. 421

18 - p. 424
19 - p. 424
20 - p. 427
21 - p. 432
22 - pp. 419-420
23 - p. 434
24 - p. 421
25 - p. 424
26 - p. 415
27 - pp. 410-411
28 - p. 411
29 - p. 412
30 - pp. 409-410
31 - p. 416
32 - p. 416
33 - p. 417
34 - pp. 414-415

35 - pp. 414-415
36 - p. 415
37 - p. 421
38 - p. 420
39 - p. 437
40 - p. 421
41 - p. 425
42 - p. 429
43 - pp. 431-432
44 - pp. 419-420
45 - p. 425
46 - pp. 412-413
47 - p. 429
48 - pp. 412-413
49 - pp. 421-422
50 - pp. 421-422
51 - p. 426

Chapter 14

1 - pp. 443-445
2 - pp. 444-445
3 - pp. 444-445
4 - p. 447
5 - p. 449
6 - p. 461
7 - pp. 448-449
8 - p. 448
9 - p. 449
10 - p. 451
11 - p. 451
12 - p. 458
13 - p. 455

14 - p. 454
15 - pp. 453-454
16 - p. 454
17 - p.456
18 - p. 459
19 - p. 458
20 - pp. 447-448
21 - pp. 448-449
22 - pp. 443-445
23 - p. 452
24 - pp. 444-445
25 - pp. 452-453
26 - pp. 447-448

27 - pp. 453-454
28 - p. 447
29 - p. 456
30 - p. 460
31 - p. 461
32 - p. 448
33 - pp. 448-449
34 - p. 461
35 - p. 461
36 - pp. 448-449
37 - p. 451
38 - pp. 444-446
39 - p. 454

Chapter 15

Appendix A

Appendix B